ONE SHOT AND THREE CHASERS

Cover design by Scott Bachmann.
Cover photo by Emma Metty

This book is a work of fiction. References to real people, events, establishments, organizations, or locales are used fictitiously, and used only to establish authenticity. All other characters and situations are created by the author and are not to be construed as real.

CorgiPress
336 Phillips St., Yellow Springs, OH 45387
www.corgipress.com
scott@scottcomics.com

First printing May 2023 ISBN 978-1-7321142-9-6

ONE SHOT AND THREE CHASERS

BY SCOTT BACHMANN

Foreword

This volume contains four plays that were all festival produced and performed in the greater Dayton, OH region. The first play is a full ninety minute two act production, the others are single acts at ten minutes.

The plays contained within are free to produce, provided the author is acknowledged and credited. For any other usage, the rights are reserved to the author.

The author would like to thank the actors and directors who took the time and hard effort to make these come alive before an audience.

These plays are dedicated to the author's sons Devin and Alex, they are his everything.

YELLOW SPRINGS ANNUAL TEN-MINUTE PLAY FESTIVAL

June 2023 will be the 13th Yellow Springs Annual Ten-Minute Play Festival. The Yellow Springs Theater Company's goal is to help writers bring their work to an audience. Originally the plays were written and directed by the writers themselves. The first festival in Yellow Springs was organized in 2009 by Holly Hudson (a former Antioch Writers' Workshop assistant director). The next year, Bob Swaney, owner of the Corner Cone in Yellow Springs, held a 10-minute-play festival. In 2011, Virgil Hervey with the assistance of Kay Reimers, producer for Center Stage Theatre Company, made this endeavor into an annual event held at the First Presbyterian Church. Hervey said "The form calls for minimal set, few actors, and minimal if any scene changes, and yet, so much can be conveyed — from humor to making a point about life — in just 10 minutes on the stage". In 2015 the event was handed off to the Yellow Springs Theater Company and we have been hosting it yearly since. We have been able to expand the festival by selecting some plays to produce ourselves. While we still focus on plays from writers in Yellow Springs and the greater Miami Valley, we also get submissions from around the world, this year as far away as Australia. After the festival of Feb 2020 we moved the festival outside due to the pandemic and pushed it back to June. The first and only year we had a theme was in 2021- topics of social injustice and experiences of those marginalized by the status quo.

FUTUREFEST

From the website at DaytonPlayhouse.com:

> Dayton Playhouse has sponsored FutureFest, a festival of new and unproduced plays since 1991, put on by a community theater run entirely by volunteers. Each year we bring you in one weekend six new unproduced plays as chosen by the FF committee from the submissions entered that year. Each play is dramatized as either a staged reading or a full dramatization. Each play is a full length play and we do not limit the subject matter. We bring the playwrights to the festival for the weekend so you can mingle with them and we have talk back sessions with them after their show. We bring in adjudicators from around the country to pick the best play and give the playwrights a professional critique in front of the FF audience. It's a play lover's dream come true, and an opportunity a playwright can't get anywhere else. FutureFest 2021 was the 30th festival and it's still going strong.
>
> Dayton Playhouse Inc. | 937-424-8477 | box.office.dayton.playhouse@gmail.com

Cross Currents

I learned about FutureFest from my wife who had volunteered to do lighting for it. I went to the festival and was stunned by the diversity and strength of the entries. It intrigued me as to how the plays were judged and selected, and I learned they regularly get 300+ submissions from playwrights around the world. As a prose writer I was also intrigued at writing that focused on dialog instead setting, and how scenes can quickly change without paragraph after paragraph of transition.

I joined the play reading committee and read over a hundred plays over three years. It was an excellent school on playwriting and how writing is received and reviewed. It taught me economy of theater and actor resources, and the tempo of the spoken word. It inspired me to write my own play which is what follows.

As a juror, I asked permission to submit my play with the head of the committee. They said it was allowed and had been done before. My play would go in as anonymous and I was not allowed to review it. I would also excuse myself from the finalists selections if my play got that far. It did.

The finalists are 12 selected plays that will be whittled down to 6 produced plays. Part of this winnowing process is contacting the authors to see if they are willing and able to participate in the festival, as all authors of plays are required to be present. My play made the list of 12, but it was decided by the committee to give it a special private performance, instead of being one of the six in the festival. The reading was performed by FF actors and presented before all of the FF play readers, performers and directors. The play was well received enough to get a standing ovation and many questions as to why it wasn't in the festival proper. I don't know why either, but many logistics go into the final six selection, and the production I was given was magnificent. The actors got all of the beats, intonations and subtlety right.

My experience with playwriting was that I loved it, but I also found the producible limits of theater too restricting. Unless you are on Broadway with a massive budget, play resources are strapped. I considered screen writing and comics/graphic novels and chose to write graphic novels. This led to dozens of works where the only limit is what an artist can draw.

CHARACTERS

Jeff York   Male, 19, Dan's son. Very laid back. Life is a pleasant ride for him. Dresses shabby but trendy.

Summer Cooper   Female, 18. Faye's daughter. Strong personality, confident. She's controlling, and quick to anger. Smartly dressed, slightly revealing.

Faye Cooper   Female, 40. Computer Technician. Not very feminine, tomboyish. Aggressive, and assertive. Likes casual clothes and sweats.

Dan York   Male 39, college professor of History. Shy, romantic, self-doubting. Clothes are neat and unnecessarily professional.

SETTING

Suburbs of a large Midwestern city.

TIME

Late Afternoon. End of Spring, around 2007.

SUMMARY

A single 40 something man with a son graduating high school meets a single 40 something woman with a daughter who has just graduated high school. As the parents adjust to dating and romance again, the children conspire to drive them apart. The rebellious children end up having their own tryst which leads to a positive pregnancy test, which the adults mistakenly think is theirs. The aftermath both drives them apart and pulls them together, making each of them come to terms with what it was like to be a single parent, or a child of one.

SCENES

ACT I

Scene 1	Both Dan and Faye's Living Rooms	Late afternoon
Scene 2	Bar/Waiting area of a restaurant	Next day, evening
Scene 3	Dan's Bedroom	Next morning
Scene 4	Dan's Living Room	2 Weeks later, early afternoon
Scene 5	Dan's Bedroom	A few days later, early evening
Scene 6	Bar/Waiting area of a restaurant	4 Weeks later, early evening
Scene 7	Dan's Bedroom	Same evening
Scene 8	Dan's Bedroom	An hour later, same evening

ACT 2

Scene 1	Both Dan and Faye's Living Rooms	Next day, evening
Scene 2	Faye's Living Room	Next day, evening
Scene 3	Dan's Living Room	Same time as last scene
Scene 4	Faye's Living Room	Following last scene
Scene 5	Hospital Waiting Room	A few hours later
Scene 6	Hospital Bed	Same time as last scene
Scene 7	Hospital Bed	An hour later

ACT I

SCENE 1

The stage is divided to show two different living rooms from modest homes in the same midwestern city. Faye's living room is on stage left, Dan's stage right. Each home is modest. Both have couches and chairs, both have doorways that lead outside, and both have a hallway door that leads off stage to the rest of the home. The rooms are similar but Faye has a TV set, and Dan does not. Both have desks with computers on them, and the desks face each other. Dan and Faye are each sitting at their desks and typing at their computers. Dan and Faye are each in their late thirties to early forties, and are dressed casually for lounging about the house. Hovering over Faye is her nineteen year old daughter, Summer, who is reading over Faye's shoulder. Dan's nineteen-year-old son, Jeff, is draped over a chair behind Dan, and is seemingly fascinated by the ceiling. It's the end of spring, late in the afternoon.

FAYE

Types intently as her daughter points at the computer screen. They appear to be arguing, but the audience can't hear them. They continue arguing while Dan and Jeff are talking.

DAN

Dan is sipping a mug of tea at the computer. He's savoring the drink.

The computer makes an alert noise.

Dan jumps in surprise, splashing the tea on his shirt.

Ah! Damn it!

Grabs some facial tissue from beside the computer and tries to blot the tea from his shirt.

The computer makes an alert noise.

JEFF

Dad. Ya got mail.

DAN

Looking for more wet spots to blot up.

I do not. Mail makes a binging sound. That was a bong. Why's it doing that? I think I broke something.

The computer makes an alert noise.

One of those thingies on the screen is shaking. I've never seen it before. Maybe I have a virus! I need your help Jeff! Fix whatever I did!

JEFF

Doesn't get up, but looks over at the screen.

Must be an Instant Message. Just click on it.

DAN

I don't know how to Instant Message. It must be for you.

JEFF

Nope. You're logged in. It's for you.

DAN

Moves the mouse and clicks carefully.

I clicked on it. I'm sure it's for you.

Beat.

Oh. It's not.

Stares at the screen in horror as he reads it.

It's that creepy matchmaker thing you set up for me. Someone read it.

SUMMER

Mom! You did not just ask him out!

FAYE

Shush. I'm terrified enough as it is.

SUMMER

I'm telling you, guys don't like it when you come on strong.

FAYE

Well I refuse to accept that you're old enough to advise me about men, so stop trying.

SUMMER

Mom. Seriously. You haven't had any in so long that you need all the help you can get.

DAN

Jeff, how do I answer back?

JEFF

Just type, and hit enter.

FAYE

Young lady I am washing your mouth out with soap.

SUMMER

Yeah well you better answer your new boy toy first. He said yes.

FAYE

Oh my god he did. I have a date. A date! Ah! What was I thinking!

DAN

Now what? Nothing's happening.

JEFF

Just wait.

DAN

Why is it an Instant message if I have to wait?

FAYE

Great, just great. He wants to go to that snooty place downtown. I don't have anything to wear! I can't do that.

SUMMER

Since when do you care what you wear? Remember the water meter guy? He won't come in the house any more after the last time he saw you.

FAYE

Reads her typing out loud as she types.

I'd love to, but can we go somewhere less formal?

SUMMER

Pushes her mom's hands away from the keyboard.

You can't say that! Men hate to be corrected. They whine.

Types and reads aloud.

I'd love to go, but can we make it Saturday?

Steps back.

There. Now we have time to shop.

DAN

It's working again! Oh my.

JEFF

What?

DAN

She said yes. I have a date this Saturday.

JEFF

With a woman?

DAN

Of course with a woman.

FAYE

Why isn't he answering? You freaked him out. I know you did.

DAN

Reads his reply out loud as he types.

Sounds wonderful. Looking forward to it.

JEFF

Oh man. Did you read her bio?

DAN

Her what? Oh, like biography? You mean that creepy form you made me fill out?
No. Should I? How do I do that?

JEFF

Well sorry old man. You just made a date with fugly hairy chick. Or a guy.

DAN

Fugly? I don't want to know what that means.

SUMMER

Tell him to meet you there at seven. That way you can show up early and sneak out if he's ugly.

FAYE

Sneak out? How did I ever raise such a horrid child?

Reads her typing out loud.

Let's meet at seven. TTFN.

DAN

The window went away! What did I do wrong? What the hell is a T T F N?

JEFF

Oh man is that old school. Ta Ta For Now. She must weigh 300 pounds and has a full mustache. And I'll bet she shows up in striped spandex and Capris. You're doomed.

DAN

That's enough. I didn't raise you to be so judgmental and mean.

Lights dim on men's half of stage, but they remain up on the women's side. Men remain on stage frozen.

FAYE

Types quickly and aggressively.

SUMMER

You've already Googled the guy. Now what?

FAYE

Well, he's a professor right? So I'm seeing what he's written.

Touches the screen, running her fingers along it as she reads.

Oh that sounds dull. "Neo-Platonism and its Impact on Aristotelian Philosophy During the Transition of Medieval Culture into the Italian Renaissance."

SUMMER

Yeah. He's a winner all right. Good thing you're as big a geek as he is.

FAYE

Geeks rule the world dear. Time to get over it. It's my mad computer skills that are paying for you to go to Baldwin Wallace next year instead of community college.

SUMMER

If you ever say mad skills again I'm going to vomit.

FAYE

Ignores her and types, pauses then reads.

Oh this one's not so bad. "Courtly Love in Contrast to Monastic Traditions, a Primer."

SUMMER

What an interesting definition of bad. Take my advice, put on the history channel, and do shots every time they say corset. You'll have a much better time.

FAYE

Apparently he just made tenure. So he must be good at something.

SUMMER

If that something were worthwhile he'd be married by now.

FAYE

He's been married. Twice. But nothing longer than a year.

SUMMER

Oh well then. That's so much better. Let me get my handcuffs. Can't let this one get away.

FAYE

Why on earth do you have handcuffs? And if you dare say sex I'm grounding you for a month with no TV.

SUMMER

They're fake mom. I bought them to go with my hotty police girl costume, the one I wore on Halloween. I've got the cap and everything. Turns out guys like to be patted down and read their rights.

FAYE

That's close enough. You're grounded until you get hot flashes.

JEFF

Lights dim on girls, rise on men. Women freeze.

Jeff is imitating his father.

Now dad, I want you to promise me one thing...

DAN

Don't mock me.

JEFF

If you find that things start to go a little too fast...

DAN

You know it's hard enough for me to tell you those things without you mocking me.

JEFF

Or if you find yourself having urges...

DAN

Yes, yes, I'll use a condom. You managed to forget the 'rules' part of the speech.

JEFF

Rule one. Never do more than kiss on the first date. Even if you think she's the one, take it slow. If you're going to give yourself you have to be sure.

DAN

I never said give yourself.

JEFF

Dad, if all that happens to me on a first date is a kiss – well there ain't gonna be a second one. That's for damn sure. All that prep work for nothing? Please.

DAN

At least tell me you're being safe.

JEFF

I'm always safe. Safe rounding for third and heading for home.

DAN

You're not to old to ground you know.

JEFF

Oh yeah I am. And you're always out cold on the couch by ten so what're you gonna do? Me, I don't even get rollin' till eleven.

DAN

Fine. Then if you're an adult, starting tomorrow, you're paying rent.

JEFF

Ah! Now that's no way to be! It's been decades since you've been out, so you gotta cut me some. All that time without some smack down release? It builds pressure on a guy, you know? I can't help it. I just gotta bust on you all at once. No need for you to go and be all harsh.

DAN

It hasn't been decades. I went out with Susan twice last year.

JEFF

Platonic arm candy - for work parties - so does NOT count.

DAN

How do you know it was just platonic? Susan and I have been colleagues for years, we've always been close.

JEFF

If she were any more frigid she wouldn't need ice in her drinks.

DAN

You will not talk about my friends that way.

JEFF

See! Friends! You admit it.

DAN

Relents.

Yeah I do. And she is an ice queen. I took her to the zoo once and she made the penguins shiver.

JEFF

Righteous! The old man goes to the rim, and swoosh, nothing but net.

DAN

If I ever spoke to my father the way you speak to me, I'd have a cherry red ass for a week, and he'd need a new belt.

JEFF

Well then lucky for you cause then it would be over. No nagging. No lectures. No blah, blah, blah, why can't you be a better kid, blah, blah blah. You have a serious gift for boring dad. You picked the perfect career.

DAN

Well I hope not too boring.

Beat.

It has been too long.

END OF SCENE

SCENE 2

> Next day, the evening. A bar in the waiting area of a restaurant.

DAN

Seated at the bar watching for Faye.

This is what I figured. This is how it goes. I'm such an idiot. I keep doing this to myself.

Looks at watch.

Fifteen minutes. I'm officially stood up. Not that I have a table yet. A table's another fifteen minutes away, which is good because if it was ready and she wasn't here then we'd lose the table, and then I'd have that going wrong. Still, it could be worse. I could have missed that parking spot and still be driving around looking for a place to park and she could show up and the table could be ready and then I'd miss both her and the table! No, that's not right. I wouldn't have a table because I wouldn't have been here to ask for one. Unless when she showed up and saw I wasn't there and that I didn't get on the list she'd put her own name down. She could be on the list right now.

Faye walks up unseen by Dan. She nervously watches Dan argue with himself.

Uh oh. What if she got here first, already got a table, and is already sitting down and wondering where I am! Did I ask the hostess? I think so. What If I said the wrong name? I could have done that. I make mistakes like that – I make all kinds of mistakes! All the time! I'm such an idiot! Why didn't I plan this better! No. I'm wrong; I mean I'm right, I mean I checked with the hostess. Yes. I'm sure.

Faye makes a face and turns around to leave.

So where is she? Maybe she can't find a parking space and is driving around and around? Maybe she got tired of not finding a space and gave up and went home? I wouldn't blame her. Maybe she saw me and ran off. I wouldn't blame her.

Faye turns back.

FAYE

Um excuse me? Hi. Are you Dan?

DAN

Huh? Oh! Yes. That's me. I'm Dan. Yes. Hi. Pleased to meet you. You're way better looking than your picture.

FAYE

Oh?

DAN

Wait, that's not what I meant. I meant you're way nicer than I thought you'd be. Not that I thought you'd be unpleasant or anything, you just surprised me. But in a good way. Oh god. I should just tape my mouth shut now before I do any more harm.

FAYE

Dan, it's ok. It's a first date, I'm a little nervous too. And I'm sorry if I kept you waiting long, I couldn't find a place to park.

DAN

I knew it. I knew it was something like that. And I wasn't waiting long. Just got here in fact. Just now. So you're right on time. Couldn't be more timely.

FAYE

Shouldn't we wait a little while before we start lying to each other?

DAN

How long should we wait?

FAYE

At least until we order. I'll pick the most expensive thing I can find, and you can pretend that's a great idea.

DAN

Ouch. That could set me back a bit in this place. How about you pretend you're full after the appetizer and you don't want a dessert?

FAYE

So you're saying I'm fat?

DAN

Oh no! I was just playing along, I didn't mean -

FAYE

Relax Dan, I know. Boy are you easy to tease.

DAN

Uh yeah. Pretty easy. A walking target really. My whole life. High school was hell.

FAYE

Wasn't great for me either – sorry! I'm already breaking my promise to my daughter! She made me swear to be nice. And no bad stories!

DAN

Daughter huh. You left that off your profile. Uh, not that I mind.

FAYE

Yeah, I do that on purpose. She just turned eighteen, and I don't look my age, so people start doing the math - and then start looking at me funny.

DAN

Not me. My son's nineteen. I'm in the same boat, only I look my age, and then some.

FAYE

Beat.

So what happened? To your wife I mean - Damn, there I go again. You don't have to answer that.

DAN

It's okay. I don't mind talking about it now. It was a car accident.

FAYE

Oh my god! I'm so sorry!

DAN

Laughs.

By car accident, I mean I was driving an old Chevy and she met a guy in a BMW and drove off with him.

FAYE

Ah. Was it recently?

DAN

No. It was ages ago, Jeff, that's my boy, he was still in kindergarten. I was running my butt off then, working full time and going to night school to get my Doctorate. She left before I was mid-way through. Screwed everything up, I had to drop out for a while. She didn't want anything tying her down which was her way of saying she wanted nothing to do with Jeff, so I got a crash course in motherhood. My sister moved in to help but she had her own life and - I'm talking too much aren't I?

FAYE

No. I like hearing someone talk about something real. I'm surrounded by men who spend half the day arguing whether 'star gates' are more realistic for space travel than 'warp drives'. Of course they spend the other half of the day trying to find new ways of doing nothing without getting caught.

DAN

Oh, so you teach college too?

FAYE

Nope. I'm down in the I.T. closet. The server room. Computer support. Geek squad. When a computer is broke, or the network is down, they managers open the little door and let us run around out of our cages. Then we wave our magic thumb drive wands to clean out the junk they've downloaded, or plug the cords back in that got pulled out, or whatever else it takes, no matter what hour of the day or night. The rest of the time they lock us back in the server cage and occasionally throw in hunks of raw meat through the mail slot. But the coffee is free, so it evens out.

DAN

Charming. But then I doubt anyone useful is ever appreciated until they're needed. Still I envy you. Technology is always changing. The only thing about history that changes is the students. Their breasts and attitudes get bigger every year, while the clothes get rattier and shorter. One day they'll all come in naked and I won't even notice.

FAYE

Yes, well it must be nice to at actually know something one day, and not have to relearn it the next. Sure there's always legacy junk to maintain, but every week there's new software patches, and if something works there's a new model that comes out that doesn't work, and there's always a new trend the front office wants to implement because they saw it at a trade show. The only thing that I can count on is that every other day something will blow up, and when one thing goes south, something else will too. It's like yawning. When one person does it, everybody does it. That's my job. Long tedious days of nothing, punctuated by pure and utter chaos.

DAN

The only thing chaotic in my life happened a week ago when the dry cleaner gave me the wrong pants. And I'm so observant I don't even notice it – not until a student pointed out that I was wearing ladies pants. I had no back pockets. Never noticed.

FAYE

Well my pants always have pockets. The more the better. I like the cargo kind with extra pockets tacked on in weird places for no reason. Damned if I don't find something to put in every one too. Which is hell come laundry day when I have to check 'em all. This is why half my pockets have chunks of white paper lint or exploded pen stains.

DAN

Makes an obvious effort to look at the lack of pockets in the dress she's wearing.

FAYE

Responds by standing up and reaching into a concealed pocket in the dress and pulls out a small screw driver and some pocket lint. She slams the screwdriver on the bar in triumph of making her point.

DAN

Stands. Reaches into his pockets and pulls out a tag. He reads the tag out loud.

Inspected by number 13. I guess these aren't my lucky pants then.

FAYE

Well now. We've created a whole new meaning for the term getting into somebody's pants.

DAN

My son would like you. That's the kind of joke he'd tell.

FAYE

My daughter would roll her eyes and gag.

DAN

Teenagers. All that energy. All that sass. And not a damn bit of sense.

FAYE

And they know everything. Won't listen to a single thing you say.

DAN

The twenties aren't any better. They don't just know everything, they're arrogant about it, strutting around the world like they own it.

FAYE

Of course we were better.

DAN

Yup. I had the smarts to marry the same woman twice. The first time was for practice, at 21. The second time, at 25, was to prove I really was the biggest idiot on the planet.

FAYE

Whole planet huh?

DAN

Yeah. Whole thing. Except for maybe Antarctica. Because Penguins are really stupid creatures. A bird that won't fly, can barely walk, and bathes in the coldest beach on earth. And what better camouflage then black on a white background? Might as well carry a sign around that says eat me.

FAYE

I'm trying to roll my eyes. Am I doing it right? It always gives me a headache when I try. And then I feel like I'm going to tip over.

DAN

Well I'm no expert - but that seems pretty good. Better stop or your face will freeze that way.

FAYE

That would be bad. If my face were going to freeze, I'd want it to be during a really pinchy cramp. That way everyone would know exactly how I feel without having to ask. Hi Faye, How are you?

Makes a pained face.

URRR.

DAN

I know that face. I used to make it a lot. I'd be running between little league, night classes, cleaning house, cutting lawns, pulling out splinters while I watched everyone around me make associate, or get tenure.

FAYE

I like to complain about my job, but work is the one thing that's been good to me. It's because I'm the quota, the minority. I always got the promotions, always got the time off that I needed. Funny though, I never got paid the same as everyone else for doing the same job.

Plus I have to wade through so much testosterone that I have to shower the second I get home. If anybody tries to tell you that geeks aren't really men, point out that video games, science fiction, and the Internet is nothing BUT explosions and porn.

DAN

Hmm. Well, I've got a doctorate, so you'd think I'd be doing well. Wrong. I'm so poor I can't afford to replace my ten-year-old TV. It has green lines running across the middle of the screen and takes five minutes to warm up before it comes on.

FAYE

It's always a pissing contest with men isn't it? I've got it harder than you. My package is bigger than yours.

DAN

Sorry. It's just that feeling sorry for myself seems to be my hobby.

FAYE

My ex hated men like you. Men had to be roughnecks, the kind that never admitted anything except when they were hungry. And women had to be demure, supportive, and in the kitchen. And if the men are talking you need to be silent unless you're showing off something they want to see.

I don't know what the hell I saw in him, or what he saw in me.

It's been fifteen years since I left him, and not a day goes by that I don't hear his bootsteps thumping in the hall. Everything he did was loud. Talking, eating, and banging on his car. For him, making noise was an art. It was his way of telling the world, here I am, deal with it! The first few years, after I left him, I used to turn up the radio and TV in every room just to cover up the creepy silence.

DAN

How did you know? I mean to end it? How did you know when it was over?

FAYE

It wasn't like that. It was more of an understanding that it never was.

DAN

I don't follow you.

FAYE

Well, I'd known for a while that it wasn't going well, but it never seemed that bad to me. There'd be these moments, just simple things when everything was right, and I'd think ah, there's more there. If only I'd try just a little bit harder those moments would burst through more often. I mean there had to be something good and strong between us to make those perfect moments happen right? But eventually I noticed they happened less often, and it got to the point when I wondered if I'd imagined them at all. Then bang, one would come along and everything felt wonderful, and I'd forget that it really wasn't.

DAN

Was he cheating on you?

FAYE

Funny, everybody asks that. Of course they're right, he was, but I didn't know it at the time. I suspected, but I never saw any proof, never could understand how this dull brained man needed more than I gave him because I couldn't figure what he would do with it. He always seemed content. What I didn't know was that he hated content. He wanted wild, daring, and that's not me. Somehow the moron found the time and the willing partners, but how? Never seemed like there was time.

It was years later that I learned a few of the sordid details, but by then I didn't care, so I didn't listen. To this day I don't know what he did or didn't do or to whom. I only know what he did to me. He lied.

DAN

My wife had the courtesy to leave me first before she cheated on me. Course it's not really cheating then, but it feels like it. I can't begin to imagine what you went through.

FAYE

The day that I knew it was over – it was odd how it played out. We were doing an installation for some company that had a lot of old equipment lying around. All kinds of meters and oscilloscopes and shortwave stuff and this guy I was working with, Clark I think his name was, or maybe that was my nickname for him because he was mousy and wore glasses like Clark Kent, and I know I saw him with a blue undershirt once - anyways, Clark's fiddling with one of these things, watching the green light pulse and jump around, and he says to me, You see these peaks? They make you think like there's some kind of signal there, but its just noise. Random noise. It's a trick of the brain to see patterns that aren't there, patterns in the spikes. And I knew that's all I had with my husband. It wasn't love; it was just the random noise of two people living together.

FAYE

Once I put that together, I understood that we were never in love. We made a child, married, got jobs, and made a lot of random noise, but it wasn't love. It was putting one foot in front of the other and going wherever that led. So I left him. Actually I didn't leave. I just told him it was over, and that he should go, and he did. But the worst thing? The worst thing was, he just said, Okay. If that's how you want it, Okay. He didn't fight. He didn't argue. Just, Okay. That's when I knew I was right. There was nothing there to lose. All the suspicion confirmed with one stupid word, Okay.

DAN

Dan stands and offers a supporting embrace, expecting rejection, but gets the opposite. They hold each other for a long beat.

Lights fade out.

END OF SCENE

SCENE 3

Dan's bedroom the next morning. Dan and Faye are asleep in Dan's bed, both nude under the covers. The room is neat except for random bits of clothing tossed around from earlier in the evening. There is a bathroom doorway stage right the same side of the bed that Faye is on. The audience shouldn't be able to see into the bathroom. There is a closed doorway stage left that leads off to the rest of the home.

Dan is sleeping on his stomach, face buried in a pillow. Faye wakes up.

FAYE

Faye fumbles around for a lamp and finds one on the end table and turns it on. A digital clock says five AM. She's groggy, hair all messed up.

Lights up from lamp.

When the light comes on she looks around, and then reacts in horror and panics.

Ahhhhhhh!!!

She lifts the sheets up and slams them down.

Ahhhhhhh!!!

DAN

Pulls the pillow over his head to drown out the yelling.

FAYE

Stops yelling for a second. Looks at Dan. Hits him hard with her pillow, and then yells again.

Ahhhhhhh!!

DAN

Sits up, protecting himself with his pillow in case she hits him again.)

What!

FAYE

I don't do this! I do not! This is not me!

DAN

Adoringly looks her up and down, and smiles.

Sorry. You're you. After last night, I'd recognize you anywhere. It's burned into my retina.

FAYE

Hits him with her pillow.

Stop undressing me with your eyes you pig!

DAN

Um – I don't have to. You're naked.

FAYE

That's not the point. You know what I mean.

DAN

Lays back down.

Ok. I'm dressing you up in my mind. But you're still wearing what I want you to wear. Nice corset by the way.

Pulls the covers up.

And could you scream again in about an hour so I can get up on time? I have a dentist appointment that was hell to schedule.

His voice drifts off to sleep as he babbles.

I missed the first appointment because of traffic and he billed me fifty bucks for it, and then he couldn't get me in for another three months. That's almost nine months since my last cleaning and just thinking about it makes my mouth feel like fuzzy tar. So I don't want to go another three months.

FAYE

This is so not happening.

DAN

Snores.

FAYE

Where are my clothes?

Tears up the bed.

DAN

Dan snatches any covers that are pulled away and does so without waking.

FAYE

Where are my clothes!

Smacks the lump of covers where Dan is.

I need to be home before my daughter wakes up! I need my clothes!

She leans over and looks under the bed. She finds one sock, a panty, and a t-shirt that is not hers. She sniffs the shirt and finds it unpleasant. She decides to put it on anyway. Faye leaves the bed and runs into the bathroom.

Light from the bathroom spills onto the stage. Running water and washing sounds are heard.

JEFF

Enters from the bedroom door stage left.

Jeff is eating a bowl of cereal as he walks. He is looking for something. He moves clothing around on the floor with his feet. He spots his Dad's wallet on the dresser so he puts the bowl down and takes some money out of the wallet.

Jeff notices the light. He looks at the bed. He looks at the light. He picks up his bowl and walks over and looks into the bathroom as he eats. He smiles approvingly.

Alright!

FAYE

Ahhhhhhh!!

Sounds of falling.

DAN

Jumps up at the screaming and falls out of bed in a tangle of covers. He crawls back up to the bed.

JEFF

Stands there eating and watching, enjoying the show.

FAYE

Slams the bathroom door closed.

Who the hell is that?

JEFF

Just me. Who the hell are you?

Turns to his dad.

I know who she is. I'm just having fun. And you're so lucky. She's not fugly at all.

FAYE

Please tell me that's your son. No don't tell me that. I can't handle that. No teenager should see me naked.

JEFF

It's Okay, you weren't really naked.

DAN

Jeff, not helping! And since when do you enter my room without knocking?

JEFF

Um, Always. This is the only bathroom with a working toilet. Since when do you let hotties run around in my old shirts?

FAYE

Do not call me a hotty!

Opens the door and throws the shirt out and slams the door closed.

JEFF

Picks the shirt up and smirks as he watches the door)

DAN

Leave!

JEFF

Shrugs and exits, giving his dad a teasing thumbs up on the way out.

DAN

Reaches over and pulls on a pair of pajama pants from the floor by the bed. He makes his way over to the bathroom door where sobbing can be heard.

I'm sorry Faye, my son can be bit crude, but he is a good kid.

FAYE

Go away. I've had enough humiliation for one morning. I don't need your pity too.

DAN

Pity? I wasn't… I mean I didn't think… Oh I don't know what I'm trying to say. He's gone. Come out and let's talk this through.

FAYE

If I was any good at talking I wouldn't be trapped in a stranger's bathroom.

DAN

Look, it's my fault too. I shouldn't have let things go so fast. You're apparently not ready, and I'm, well I don't know how to handle upset people. Usually I just flee the room. I hate parties; never go to them if I can help it. Actually most people would expect me to be the one hiding out in the john.

I don't know what to say to make this better. I didn't want to hurt you. Or scare you. I really like you. I really, really like you. And I don't do this kind of thing either. Honestly. I dated my wife for six months before we did anything, and I was a virgin when we married. Oh god, shut up Dan. No one wants to hear this stuff.

FAYE

Opens the door a crack.

I do. I like hearing you talk. You're honest. Even when you're trying to lie you seem to have a way of letting the true fall out.

DAN

Thanks. I think. And I like listening to you too. You're funny, and brave, and confident.

FAYE

Even when I'm hiding in a bathroom?

DAN

Yes. And you know who you are. And you know who you're not. Me? I don't know anything about me. I just kind of fall through life, one foot in front of the other, doing whatever comes next, and no idea where I'm heading.

FAYE

Opens the door more.

Dan. I don't really know. It's all an act. Bluster. I never know what I'm doing.

DAN

Then, can I hide in the bathroom with you?

FAYE

Laughs. Reaches out and pulls him in.

Now I remember how this happened. I really, really, like you to.

DAN

Um, should I cover my ears? You're naked again. And you scream really loud.

FAYE

Depends. You going to give me a reason to?

Lights down on the room leaving the bathroom lights on and shadows from the bathroom embracing. After a beat, lights out.

END OF SCENE

SCENE 4

Dan's living room. Two weeks later. The room is the same as scene one, but the stage no longer needs to be divided.

Lights come up with Jeff and Summer on opposite ends of the couch. Jeff looks comfortable with his feet up on a coffee table. Summer sits cross-armed, and wears a look that suggests the room is crawling with bugs and she doesn't want to touch them. Dan is standing by the front door with several suitcases beside him. Faye is possessively straightening Dan's shirt and making him presentable.

SUMMER

Mom! Why do I have to stay here? I'm old enough to stay home by myself. I'm old enough to rent my own apartment!

FAYE

Well until you do, you live under my rules, and I'm not leaving you home alone.

SUMMER

I'm older than he is!

DAN

And you get better grades. But your mother is right. The last time she left you home alone you threw a party so big she had to rent two steam cleaners and an exorcist to fix the damage.

SUMMER

Mom! That's private stuff!

FAYE

And Jeff locked himself out of the house once and had to spend the night at an all you can eat diner.

JEFF

It's not really all you can eat. They cut you off.

FAYE

We figured you two can take care of each other, and it's a good way to get know each other. And it's only for three nights.

28

DAN

Wistfully.

Three nights on the beach! Cabanas. Margaritas. Late night swims…

Gives Faye a playful squeeze.

SUMMER

Oh gross! It's bad enough hearing you through the walls.

JEFF

I just blast the stereo.

SUMMER

Mom!

FAYE

Summer. You were the one encouraging me to get back on the bike so I don't want to hear you complain if I ride it around a few times.

SUMMER

I meant get a little, not shack up! This is so crazy. Oh god that's it isn't it? This is a practice to see if we can get along. You're going to all Brady Bunch on us and get married and then I'll have to share a bathroom with mister I-only-need-one-pair-of-socks-a-week.

JEFF

Wiggles his toes.

It's easier than trying to find a match.

DAN

Not helping Jeff. And Summer, I know we've only been dating a few weeks, but neither of us has had a vacation in years. You don't need to read anything into it.

SUMMER

Mom, you haven't seen sunlight in years, and now you're going to the Caribbean? You might as well be picking out paint swatches!

FAYE

This room could use a touch of blue.

SUMMER

Mom!

DAN

She's definitely got your voice. Now kids, you have our cell phone numbers, and there's emergency money in the coffee can. And an emergency Jeff is not Pizza. You have food money, and the cars have gas. Is there anything I forgot?

FAYE

House arrest anklets. We could still run out and get a set.

JEFF

Those invisible alarms for dogs don't work too well. My buddy Jake and I put the collars on once and dared each other to run the fence.

Shakes like he's being shocked.

Not a problem.

SUMMER

I am so not responsible if the fur ball here pees on the rug.

FAYE

That's enough Summer. I haven't taken a vacation in five years. I'm overdue. And after all we've been through; you owe me at least one weekend of good behavior. So make it work.

DAN

And Jeff. Don't be yourself. Behave. Please.

JEFF

No problem. Have fun. Don't do anything I'd do. You're too old. Heart attack.

FAYE

He has your honesty. Okay kids. Bye.

DAN/SUMMER

Bye.

DAN

Walks out with the suitcases. Faye seems hesitant to leave. Dan walks back in and drags her out. Dan returns again.

Bye. Love you. And Beer is not an emergency.

Exits.

SUMMER

That was dramatic. Ok. Here are the ground rules. You don't talk to me or mess
with my things, and I'll ignore you. And shower. You need to shower. I can smell
you from here. I don't want to smell boy all weekend.

JEFF

Girl. You got issues. All of them. Whatever. As long as I've got the TV we're fine.

SUMMER

And shower, I'm serious.

JEFF

This big sister thing you're doing here isn't working for me. This is my house. My
couch. You don't get to push me around in my house.

SUMMER

Well now part of it is mine so deal.

JEFF

Huh.

Ponders something as Summer watches.

What you said before, that's not a good thought. What if the love birds hook up
Vegas style? You know, a drive thru quickie wedding with Elvis and a convertible?
Then I'm really stuck with you. That I can't cope with. I mean you're very easy on
my eyes, but my ears won't take it.

SUMMER

See, this is why you need to not talk. Because I can't unhear what you just said. Oh,
I so cannot have you for a brother!

JEFF

Mutual.

Long beat as both of them sulk.

SUMMER

I have a plan.

JEFF

Ignores her.

SUMMER

I said I have a plan.

JEFF

Ignoring her. Turns on the TV.

TV sounds.

SUMMER

Gets up, stands in front of TV.

I. Said. I. Have. A. Plan!

JEFF

You used to have some rules too. I was following them. Now why don't you follow them and move.

SUMMER

Pay attention!

Turns off TV.

TV sound ends.

You and I, we need to split them up, for good.

JEFF

If you're going to talk, you could at least turn around so I can watch your best side.

SUMMER

Exactly! That's my plan. You just keep thinking with your little head. We can use that to our advantage.

JEFF

I thought I was clear; show me the side without the mouth.

SUMMER

If your dad thought we were having sex, what would he do?

JEFF

Laughs.

Have another fake heart attack. Lots of gasping and stuttering. Once I made him so mad all he could do was squeak.

SUMMER

My mom would scream until the windows shattered.

Summer wags her finger like she's lecturing Jeff.

But they'd break up just to keep us apart.

JEFF

If all you wanted to do was get into my jeans, all you had to do was ask. And then -
NOT SAY ANOTHER WORD 'CAUSE IT AIN'T HAPPENING.

SUMMER

Ew. No. I didn't mean for real. We fake it.

Summer waves Jeff off dismissively.

You wouldn't be my type if every guy in the world jumped off a cliff and all the
vibrators in the world ran out of batteries.

JEFF

Yeah? Your mom must have screwed a big ass snake, 'cause you've got the spitting
venom trick down cold.

SUMMER

Look. All we need to do is let them catch us pretending to do it when they come
home. If I don't vomit and give it away, we win. We won't have to see each other
ever again.

JEFF

Does this plan involve you being naked? Because we may need to practice this a
few times to get it right.

SUMMER

Forget it. I need another plan. I don't want you thinking about my goodies when
you're jerking off.

JEFF

Goodies? Goodies. That's a new one to me.

SUMMER

God I'm so stupid. No one would ever believe I'd go anywhere near you except
with a can of mace! I'm done with you. I'll think of something on my own.

JEFF

Good. Now step away from the tube.

SUMMER

Throws something at him, and stalks out. The next line is delivered from offstage.

Exits the doorway leading to the inner house.

I hate you!

JEFF

And there's pizza in the fridge. Make sure you put some in your mouth. Keep it occupied.

Lights down.

END OF SCENE

SCENE 5

> Dan's bedroom a few days later. Lights come up with
> Summer in an oversized T-shirt sitting on Jeff who is
> lying on the bed. Jeff is wearing jeans and nothing else.

JEFF

No way. I'd be on the top. I know it. You know it.

SUMMER

You are not getting on me for any reason. And I know you like it. I can feel you through your pants. So shut up and just LOOK like you like it.

JEFF

I'll make a deal. You shut up, and I promise I'll like it.

SUMMER

You're not funny, you know that right? And you're not helping.

JEFF

What's not helping are the clothes. Nobody screws with clothes on unless it's TV.

SUMMER

They're parents. They will be too busy freaking out to think about that. And I am not getting naked in front of your father.

JEFF

Oh, but you would for me? Progress.

SUMMER

Get it through your thick skull, I don't like you.

JEFF

Liar. 'Cause it's not cold in here.

SUMMER

> Crosses her arms over her chest and jumps out of the bed.

I hate you. This was a stupid idea.

JEFF

Blah blah blah. Hate, venom, stupid, blah blah blah. God. You're so frigid you make penguins want to go to the zoo.

SUMMER

What?

JEFF

I screwed up the joke. You know what I mean.

SUMMER

Yeah well I've slept with five different guys. I'm sure the only girls you've been with have staples in them.

JEFF

Try twenty. And I get no complaints, and lots of repeat business. In fact I'm seeing a sweet one right now. She might be the one. She's the quiet type.

SUMMER

Liar.

JEFF

You're the liar. There's no way you found five deaf guys in this city.

Off stage, the sound of a door opening and closing, and faint conversation.

SUMMER

Panics for a beat then jumps into bed beside Jeff and yanks the covers over both of them. Struggling is seen under the covers, and then her T-shirt is tossed out of the bed.

Long beat, then both of their heads poke out from the covers.

Long beat.

Off stage the conversation ends and a door is heard opening and closing.

I think they left! Why did they leave?

JEFF

You really are beautiful. Too bad I hate you. This would have been great.

SUMMER

Of course it would have been great. I'm not one of your inflatable fantasies.

JEFF

You sure? This looks like where I'm supposed to blow you up.

SUMMER

Screams and giggles.

Stop that! You're insane you little animal. Stop it. Do not do that.

JEFF

That damn mouth again.

> *He kisses her. She struggles and slowly relents. He lets her go.*
> *Long beat as they stare at each other.*

I finally got you to shut up.

SUMMER

Jerk.

JEFF

Squeals with laughter.

No tickling! Cheat! Help! Help!

Lights down.

END OF SCENE.

SCENE 6

4 weeks later, same setting as scene 2, the bar in the waiting area of restaurant.

Lights come up with Dan seated facing Faye. They are dressed up for a night out and the act starts with them in mid conversation.

FAYE

So what's the proper gift for a one month anniversary, chewing gum, or fast food gift certificates?

DAN

We have to be married to have an anniversary. This is more of a celebration.

FAYE

I fail to see how coming back here qualifies as a celebration. We've been waiting twenty minutes already.

DAN

I'm sorry, we can go somewhere else. I just thought that going back to where we met would be romantic.

FAYE

Sweet yes. Romantic? Not so much. Especially not after the sunsets and swim up bars in Cancun.

DAN

Weren't you the one who told me you didn't have a romantic bone in your body?

FAYE

No. I simply said it was broken down and rusting from lack of use.

DAN

Very well then, let's check and see if it works at all. Name your favorite romantic movie.

FAYE

Star Wars. You?

DAN

Casablanca. But Star Wars? Seriously?

FAYE

Of course I'm serious.

DAN

Fine. Name one thing romantic in it.

FAYE

Only one? Lonely boy sees the image of a beautiful princess begging for help. He leaves home, family, and friends to find her. He risks his life over and over again to save her. In saving her he gets a kiss and then he rushes off to save the rest of the world for her, and she gives him a medal and a smile at the end. He risked everything for love, and won against the impossible.

But then there's your film. An old grumpy coward sees his ex and sends her away to America with another guy just so he can remain living in sin with his effete French friend.

DAN

That's… Well it's just not right.

FAYE

Would you rather me go into all of the sexual symbolism in Star Wars? There are the phallic symbols of R2D2, the X-wing fighter, and the light sabers themselves. Gotta love growing and glowing rods. Then there's the whole trench approach. The one that leads to shooting the missile into the Death Star's hole followed by an orgasmic explosion. It's a miracle the movie wasn't R rated.

DAN

You're shameless. I'll never be able to watch that movie again.

FAYE

Besides, Casablanca was going to be cast with Ronald Regan, and we all know what happened to him, became president and started what program?

DAN

Star Wars.

FAYE

Yes Star Wars. And let this be a lesson to you. Never debate anything with a geek.

DAN

Wouldn't I have to get a word in edgewise for this to qualify as a debate?

FAYE

Well if we're still together on our second monthly celebration, I'll let you have a word or two.

DAN

How generous. And I'll be kind in return and let you pay for the meal.

FAYE

Dan, I make more than you. You really should let me pay for all of the meals.

DAN

Good thing my ex-wife took my ego away in the divorce settlement.

FAYE

Her loss, because she left the best parts behind.

DAN

And what would those parts be? Since no one else has ever seemed to notice them before you.

FAYE

Well you like me. You let me win. You have a sense of humor. And you like me.

DAN

You said that twice.

FAYE

It's twice as important.

DAN

You know what I really like about you?

FAYE

Do you want the clean or the dirty answer?

DAN

The sincere one.

FAYE

I don't know really.

DAN

You live like you love life. A little cynical, but happy. Most people are trying to ignore life, or escape it. You grab it by the throat and make it do what you want.

FAYE

So I'm a pit bull?

DAN

You're changing the subject.

Everyone lost in my office pool. No one had us lasting this long.

FAYE

Well at least your coworkers could imagine us going out. I'm the only girl in the IT department. That means every guy has me a on a pedestal, and thinks I'm theirs, or else I'm gay. Dating outside the herd? Never occurs to them.

DAN

Anybody I should be jealous of? Anybody I should tease you about?

FAYE

I did go out with Steve once. He's a sales rep, so not really one of our guys, but he's always around because his stuff never works right. He hangs around so much we gave him a desk with a nameplate. Of course we made sure nothing worked, including the adjustable chair.

DAN

Is this a setup for a joke about how well he works or something? Because I don't need to hear about that.

FAYE

Oh no, he worked rather well - until I figured out he was married.

DAN

So is this a story that goes in the jealousy or tease you category?

FAYE

Go ahead and try to tease me. You'll find out why Steve changed companies and doesn't come around anymore. And walks with a limp.

DAN

You're a very scary person.

FAYE

It's a necessity. I'm a girl in a boy's world.

DAN

That's odd, because when I started out my department was all men and the student body was all male, now half the department and most of the students are female.

FAYE

Sure, 'cause it's not engineering or computer science. We're still under 3% industry wide. And the female managers in the rest of the company? Bitches.

DAN

Well the women I work worth with are the best. They are the serious ones and the considerate ones. The men on the other hand, they are the picky prima donnas.

And the 'A' students? They're all female. It's the boys who sleep in class.

FAYE

Ah progress.

So why is it we don't talk like this more often? Why do we have to go out to talk?

DAN

Because it's rude to have sex in public so we have nothing left to do except talk.

FAYE

So is that all I am to you Dan? Someone to have sex with?

DAN

No, no, no. That's not what I meant. I was joking.

FAYE

Yeah but all jokes have a bit of truth in them. That's what makes them funny.

DAN

Well after a bit of a dry spell we both deserve to act like teenagers, or newlyweds. That's not such a bad thing is it?

FAYE

No. It's not. I just want to be sure that there's something more between us.

DAN

Aside from telling you there is, how can I prove it? Because there is more. You're the only person I've felt comfortable around since…

FAYE

Since your wife?

DAN

Oh hell no. She never made me comfortable. Anxious, nervous, but never comfortable.

FAYE

Then who?

DAN

My first love. The girl down the road from me. We'd walk to school together and it was the only time I ever felt like the world was a nice place to be in.

FAYE

So the world's a nice place to be in when I'm around?

DAN

Sure. Even better, it's nice when you aren't around, because I know you're out there. Makes everything right.

FAYE

I'm not that wonderful a person. And I don't belong on a pedestal.

DAN

It would be nice if one day I could make you feel the way I do.

FAYE

That's not what I meant. I do love you. That's what scares me. I'm scared to love anyone.

What happens when that day comes and you wake up and realize I'm not that special? Well what happens is that you'll leave, and I'll be walking around again with a hole where my heart should be. I can't do that again. Ever.

DAN

Ah. So better to be miserable than to be, well, miserable.

FAYE

I didn't say it made sense. That's just the way it is.

DAN

Very angry.

So what's the point in having dinner? We should just go back home and screw. Nice and meaningless. All just fun and games. No one getting hurt because nothing matters.

FAYE

Dan.

DAN

What. I'm wrong? What's wrong is you trying to push me away.

You need to take a look at yourself and decide what you want out of life, because I'm not going to keep chasing someone who doesn't want to be cared about. I've done that. And I'm not doing that again.

Come on. Let's go. I'm taking you home.

FAYE

Don't. I'll call a cab.

DAN

I see. So are we over then?

FAYE

No. But I think we need to slow down.

DAN

Fine.

Dan stands up and puts on his coat.

I'll call you tomorrow.

Dan exits without looking back.

FAYE

Covers her mouth.

Lights down.

END OF SCENE.

SCENE 7

Dan's bedroom same evening. The room is the same as before.

Summer is leaning on the doorway to the bathroom. Jeff is pacing in the farthest corner of the room. Both are fully dressed. Both look serious and upset. Summer has a plastic pregnancy test stick in her hand that she's staring at.

SUMMER

Looks at the test again.

I'm definitely pregnant.

JEFF

It's only been two weeks. Those things aren't that accurate.

SUMMER

Yes they are. And I can feel it. I'm pregnant.

JEFF

It's not possible. You take the pill.

SUMMER

Sounds like she's lying.

Yeah well, that doesn't seem to matter does it?

JEFF

Well then it's from before we -

SUMMER

- There's no before Jeff. I haven't been with anyone. Not in a while. It's yours.

JEFF

Oh.

Stops pacing. He's fighting back a lot of anger. He visibly lets it go. His humor sounds forced.

Well at least he'll be handsome. He'll have your smile.

SUMMER

He?

45

JEFF

She?

Looks away, staring off into space.

Doesn't matter.

SUMMER

Shit. What are we gonna do? I can't be pregnant. I'm not screwing up my life. I am not my mom!

JEFF

Well I'm not my dad. I'm not getting married. Not over this.

Turns to look at Summer.

You could have-

SUMMER

- Don't you say IT! Don't you dare say it!

Hits the wall with her hand a few times.

I won't do that. I won't!

JEFF

A kid needs a family. A father AND a mother.

SUMMER

You think I don't know that? You really think I don't know that?

Beat.

Damn! I've got my acceptance letters already! I busted my ass to get in! I'm not going to some damn community college!

JEFF

So wait a year.

SUMMER

A year? Try twenty!

Long beat.

JEFF

Does anyone else know?

SUMMER

Waves the test around.)

No genius. Just you. Just now.

Gestures at the bathroom.

And fix your damn spare bathroom! I hate being in here!

Summer's trying to not cry.

JEFF

We tried to fix it, but the pipes are messed up. Hard water or something like that. You have to take the wall apart, and Dad's terrible with tools, and the plumber charges too much.

Hey. Until you two came along there wasn't any need to fix it! In fact I liked sharing. It gave me and Dad a reason to talk in the morning. No yelling about grades and shit.

Long beat.

Look, I don't want to get married - but I'll help out. I mean it.

SUMMER

Well that makes it all better.

JEFF

What do you want from me? I'm just being honest.

SUMMER

Yeah. You're always honest. It sucks. You could try lying. Tell me everything's going to be alright.

JEFF

Maybe it will be. My dad and I did OK. It's not the end of the world.

SUMMER

Yes it is. My world anyway.

I'm such an idiot.

JEFF

Jeff crosses the room to be next to Summer. He puts his hand on her shoulder. She doesn't react.

You're a straight A student. You're mother's a brain. You know how to work the cable remote. You're not an idiot.

SUMMER

You're getting better at lying.

JEFF

Jeff has a hard time talking, for what seems to be the first time in his life.

And earlier... I meant that... I don't want to – well - get married... I mean, yet. Maybe after we know each other... it could change. You never know.

Jeff pulls himself together.

I mean miracles can happen. I actually showered for you. On a Wednesday.

SUMMER

Smiles and wipes her eyes.

You're sweet in your own deranged way.

Summer looks at Jeff as if seeing him for the first time.

I don't want to get married either. Career, kids, school, no time to sleep or smile. I don't want that for me. I don't.

JEFF

We'll work something out.

SUMMER

There's nothing to work out. This is my problem, not yours. We were just screwing around. Using each other. It didn't mean a damn thing.

Jeff steps away from Summer as if struck.

You have a girlfriend you're cheating on. How do I know you won't cheat on me? I don't want there to be a "we".

JEFF

Yeah, we WERE messing around. But THIS is different. Way different. No boy of mine is EVER going to grow up alone.

He. She. Whatever. No way.

SUMMER

Great. If he needs help rolling a joint instead of tying his shoes, you'll be the one I call.

JEFF

Jeff seems about to yell, then stops and smiles instead.

That's the viper I know. Always ready to fight the whole world. You're tough. Fearless. You can do this, I know it.

Jeff clasps Summer's chin in his hand and makes her look at him.

We can do this.

SUMMER

Summer takes his hand away from her face, establishing her space, but then Summer takes Jeff's hand and holds it.

I'm sorry. That was exceptionally cruel of me. You've been an angel.

The tears start to come back and she fights them again.

Shit. Sorry. I'm just sorry. I'm sorry I got you into this. I'm sorry I did this to me. Shit.

JEFF

Jeff is visibly uncomfortable and shrugs it off.

No worries babe. No worries.

Sound of a door opening/closing off stage.

Worries! Your Mom's home early!

Summer searches for the trashcan while Jeff check's the hall. Summer buries the test in the trash and both rush out of the room.

FAYE

Faye enters the bedroom looking tired. She's carrying a grocery bag with something in it.

She puts her keys and purse down on the dresser.

She stares at the bag then looks around as if worried she'll be seen.

She works up her courage and enters the bathroom carrying the bag.

FAYE

Long beat.

The sound of toilet flushing and hand washing off stage.

Faye re-enters bedroom carrying a pregnancy test and staring at it in disbelief. She has the box in her other hand and she reads the instructions again.

Clear. I was so sure. Damn.

She sits down on the bed, and looks like all of the life has drained out of her. She's still staring at the test.

Why am I not happy? It's dangerous to be pregnant at my age.

And I'm over all of that. I'm done with all the diapers and the snot and the tears and the report cards and the deserts I'm supposed to bring. I want to be able to sleep at night, no crying, no worrying, no sick children needing their mommy.

Faye wipes her eyes.

Guess I was hoping for something else. Would it be so awful to get a second chance? I know what I'm doing now, it wouldn't be so hard.

Faye runs her hand through her hair and shakes her head.

Wow. It just felt so real. I was so sure. But no.

Throws the box in the trash. Beat. She reconsiders and shoves the box deeper into the trash.

Empty nest syndrome. That's what it is. My baby's all grown up.

Faye begins pantomiming what's she's saying.

She never sat still. Always squirming and burping, crying and laughing. She was so small. She needed me for everything. That jerk I married didn't need me, but she did. Her big smile when I wiped her nose. The way she giggled in the bath. Water and soap was everywhere but in the tub or on Summer. She used to catch the shower rain and try to put it back. She set Ken on fire and threw him out of her tree house, just so Barbie could fly down and save him - wearing a piece of my scarf as a cape. That tree house was more bent nails and splinters then wood, but we built it. I want to build another one.

Exits. Lights out.

END OF SCENE.

SCENE 8

Dan's bedroom an hour later, the same evening. The room is the same as before. No one is in the room. There is a note on the bed. Dan enters.

DAN

Reads the note out loud.

Took kids out for Pizza. They looked miserable and guilty. Not sure what's up. Look for broken things around the house. May stop for ice cream too, I need chocolate. Love Faye.

Sighs.

Miserable? They've been getting along so well! Wonder what's happened. Probably nothing. They're teenagers. Nothing they do makes sense. Then again, what if it's us? Maybe we're going too fast for them – lord knows I've made that mistake before. That's got to be rough on them. It's rough on me. Come to think of it, I haven't really discussed any of this with Jeff. He always acts out when I'm dating. You'd think I remember that.

Dan suddenly shudders.

Huh. I haven't been alone like this for a while. House quiet. Faye's never quiet. It's funny how quickly we get used to things. I was alone for years, and now I've forgotten what it's like. Then again -

Picks up a piece of Faye's clothing.

- it feels like we just met an hour ago. Yes. Just an hour. Damn. This house feels creepy empty.

Dan crumples up the note and throws it at the trashcan. Misses. He walks over and puts it in the trash. He does a double take on the trash. He reaches in and pulls out a pregnancy test.

Oh.

He's shocked to find it, and then he reads the results.

Oh! Oh my! This is so. Well. Hum. This is not... Wow.

He sits down on the bed in the same spot that Faye was an hour ago. He stares into space for a beat, his face blank.

Faye's having my child.

END OF ACT.

ACT II

SCENE 1

> Opens in the divided set from Act 1 Scene1 of Faye's and Dan's living room. Faye's room has changed to be sparser of personal furnishings, while Dan's should be more cluttered with Faye's belongings like nick-knacks, tchotchkes, and pillows.
>
> Faye is in her own house with Summer. Faye is standing and appears upset while Summer is sitting at the computer. Summer is sitting backwards in the chair, facing her mom and with her back to Dan's half of the stage.
>
> Dan and Jeff are in Dan's home. Dan is puttering around his hose, straightening things, nervous. Jeff is half asleep on the couch, all sprawled out.
>
> It's evening. The day after the Act break. Lights are focused on the women, while the men are in dim light.

> FAYE

> *Breathless rant. Hands gesturing and body pacing as she talks.*

Right after tea. He gives me some damn pastry thing - bought at some damn yuppie place that makes silly things with icing and sprinkles – and not normal sprinkles, the kind in weird pastel colors – and each pastry is a zillion calories just for looking at it, a diabetic would die from smelling it – and he takes the evil thing out a box, which is of course covered in gold leaf and wrapped to hell and back with ribbons - and he lays the things out on expensive china - not the plastic stuff he usually uses because all that man ever eats is take out - and then he pours out some god awful tea with a weird name that doesn't even taste like tea - and then he sat back - all smiles – just smiling for like forever - like I had something in my teeth – and then he asks me – just blurts it out, no warm up, no lead in - just WHAM.

> *She takes a long breath, tries to calm down from hyper to sober.*

He asks me to marry him.

> *Beat.*

No ring. We get to shop for that tomorrow. He's got that trip all planned out. Anything I want. But oh, that doesn't matter; it's our love that matters, which is fine and all – I don't give a damn about diamonds – but no ring…

FAYE

Beat.

That means he didn't plan this. No hints, no warnings, no trips to the mall where we accidentally look at jewelry when he's pretending to shop for a watch, no jokes about great places for honeymoons, no long speeches about love and all that other crap men do when they think they are being clever - none of it! He just asks me to marry him. And, OH. NO need to answer right away, oh no, he doesn't want an immediate answer. We can take it SLOW.

Very sarcastic.

Slow as we want. As long as we're F. U. C. K. I. N. G. engaged!

Drops to a chair, spent.

Lights change to focus on men.

DAN

Pacing, agitated.

I'm thinking of painting. We've never painted. No one has white walls anymore. Everything is colors and textures and designs. They have five cable channels devoted to messing with your house, and not a single show raves about white walls. Feathers or hay glued to the plaster is fine, but white is just -

Tries to think of something, fails.

Well it's not good. All we have are white walls, every last one.

Stares at one wall.

Okay, not white, but dingy white because I don't know how to wash a wall. Years of grime. So they need paint. Make the place new again. Different. That's what we need. Different. Faye should choose. Let Faye make her mark. Make this her home too. Yes, yes, yes. Paint. Answer to everything. Paint over it.

Drops into a chair, and changes moods from upbeat to morose.

Oh whom I kidding. There isn't enough paint in a hardware store to make this dump a home. I should take a match to the whole thing. Or sell it. Start over. New house, new yard, new life. Space for a cradle –

Interrupts himself.

Couch. God do I need I new couch. Can't paint a couch!

Lights focus on women.

SUMMER

So. What did you say?

FAYE

Nothing. I couldn't say anything. First time in my life my mouth didn't move. Didn't even scream. It was awful. He kept looking at me, waiting for something. Anything.

Beat.

So I nodded.

SUMMER

A yes nod, or an OK I'll think about it nod?

FAYE

I don't know! My head moved. All on its own. I could have been one of those stupid dogs in the back window of a car; I don't know how I nodded!

SUMMER

What did he say?

FAYE

Nothing. He just nodded back. Then we drank crappy tea in silence. Then we went to bed and had crappy, awkward sex.

SUMMER

Beat.

So, did you nod instead of moan?

FAYE

You're not helping!

Lights focus on men.

JEFF

Jeff sits up.

So Dad. Since you're in a good mood - or whatever you call this strung out buzz ya got going – I've got something to ask you.

DAN

Dan is distracted, lost in his thoughts, not hearing Jeff.

Huh? Oh yeah. Sure. Anything. Ask me anything. Whatever you want. Talking is good for the soul. We don't talk enough! Why don't people ever say what they mean anymore? It's a tragedy really. Welcome to the future. Computers came in, talking went out.

DAN

Realizes what he sounds like.

Beat.

Sorry. It's been a long week.

JEFF

Creeped out.

Right.

Beat.

Dan is impatiently waiting.

Jeff gets up his nerve again.

So Summer and me... There's something you need to know...

Beat.

Something kinda happened.

DAN

Was anybody hurt?

JEFF

Uh, no -

DAN

Anything broken? You haven't broken anything in awhile. It's OK, I forgive you.

JEFF

Dad! Nothing's broken! Everybody's fine. Well mostly. Ugh. This is hard. Summer's gonna kill me for telling you.

DAN

So, it's a secret is it... and Summer confided in you? That's a good sign. A very good sign.

JEFF

What are you talking about?

DAN

I think I know your secret.

JEFF

You know?

DAN

About the Baby? Yeah. I know. I found out by accident. No surprise though that I'm the last to be told. I don't think I ever know what's going on until it's all over.

JEFF

Ok. Wasn't expecting that. So, what? Are you Ok with it?

DAN

Of course I am! Why wouldn't I be!

JEFF

Shocked reaction.

A lot of reasons! But hey, you're Okay with it. So that's good. Real good.

DAN

Very good. It's a little sudden all of this, but it's good. We all like each other, so it'll just bring us all closer together. One big happy family.

JEFF

One big happy family?

DAN

Yeah. I proposed to Faye.

Big contagious grin.

I asked her to marry me. Right there. In the kitchen. Warmed her up with fancy deserts. Got on my knees and everything.

JEFF

Stunned.

Why? Because of the baby?

DAN

Of course. It's the right thing to do.

JEFF

Look of horror.

It is?

Manages a lame smile.

Thanks?

Lights focus on women.

SUMMER

Faye is distant, lost in thought. Summer looks like she's been trying for a while to get her attention.

Mom. Mom. Mom!

Faye looks up at last.

I need to say something. I know this isn't the best time, but -

FAYE

I don't have any money.

SUMMER

What? No. I don't need any money – well actually I could use a twenty – but that's -

FAYE

Summer Elaine Cooper! I have enough problems without you getting all needy on me!

SUMMER

No, this is important, real important, and I should have said something sooner -

FAYE

It damn well better be important. I am so not in the mood!

SUMMER

Never mind.

FAYE

Don't you start on me! Don't give me any of that passive-aggressive teenage bullshit. I can't deal with you right now. Whatever it is, work it out on your own. You're a grown woman, start acting like one!

SUMMER

How? Like you? Then fine! I will!

Storms off stage

Exits the door leading to the inner part of the house.

FAYE

Screams in frustration.

Kids!

Throws something.

It's always about them!

Fade lights on entire scene.

END SCENE.

SCENE 2

> Faye's living room the next day.
> Lights are dim, no one is home.

JEFF

Jeff knocks on the front door.

Hello? Summer? Summer!

Knocks on front door.

Hello? Ok. I'm using the key in the fake rock that I'm not supposed to know about.

Sound of door unlocking. Jeff enters.

Jeff fumbles for the light switch, knocks something over.

Lights on.

Jeff wanders about, looking for hints as to where Summer might be.

Hello?

Jeff exits using the door that leads into the home.

Calls out from off stage.

Summer? Summer! Summer?

FAYE

Faye is coming home from work. She's upset to find the front door is unlocked.

Enters from front door.

Summer! You get down here this instant! You left the lights on and the door open again! Any strange guy could just come in here and –

JEFF

Jeff enters from the bedroom.

-and what? Summer took four years of Tae Kwan Doe; she can kick any guy's ass.

FAYE

Jeff. What are you doing in my house?

JEFF

Looking for Summer. She won't answer her cell, her email, nothing.

FAYE

What did you do to make her mad?

JEFF

Nothing.

FAYE

This is Summer were talking about. Summer collects grudges the way other girls collect shoes. Are you sure you didn't do something?

JEFF

Oh I did something alright. I just didn't do anything to make her mad.

FAYE

Fine, don't tell me then.

She sits on her couch. Takes off her shoes.

Since you're here, how about making yourself useful and getting me a beer from the fridge.

JEFF

Little early in the day for that isn't it?

FAYE

Jeff. Not all off us get up at three in the afternoon and call it morning, I've been up since five. I've been yelled at all day by bosses who wouldn't know their own name if it wasn't on their ID Badges. I'm tired, it's my house, and I want a beer.

Faye glares at Jeff.

I shouldn't have to justify myself in my own house.

JEFF

Fair enough. Mind if take one?

FAYE

Are you twenty-one?

JEFF

Are you my mom?

FAYE

No. No I'm not. Not yet…

Damn. Bring me two. You only get one.

JEFF

Back in a bit.

Jeff exits the door to the inner part of the house.

FAYE

Rubs her own feet. Stops. Hunts around for the TV remote and finds it shoved into the couch. She tries to turn on the TV with the remote. Nothing happens. She smacks the remote, and then shakes it. Nothing happens. She opens the battery compartment and shifts the batteries around, then tries again. Nothing happens.

She throws the remote at the TV.

Jeff enters.

Jeff emerges with a single glass and two bottles of beer. He hands Faye the glass and sets one of the bottles next to her on an end table.

He starts to drink from the remaining bottle in long swigs. Faye pours her beer and sips it.

They stare at each other.

Faye tries to break up the awkward silence.

What should I be doing? Right now. If I was your mother.

JEFF

Jeff doesn't like the question.

Dunno. Telling me to do my homework?

More awkward silence as they drink. Jeff can't sit still, so he fidgets with things he finds around the room. Faye watches him.

FAYE

We've got nothing in common.

JEFF

Nope.

FAYE

Hard to believe.

You're father and I never stop talking.

JEFF

That's not hard to believe. Summer never to shuts up, and you're her ma.

FAYE

True. She doesn't ever shut up. Always has to be the center of attention. No matter how much attention I give her, it's never enough.

She kicked the whole time she was inside me too.

JEFF

Did it hurt?

FAYE

No. Well when I had to pee it was awful, but no, it didn't hurt.

JEFF

Did she cry a lot?

FAYE

I wish. She skipped crying and went straight to screaming. She could spit out her pacifier and scream at the same time. It was like an air horn. And when she belched you could feel the ground shake.

JEFF

She can still do that. We had a contest. I'd never been beat before I met her.

FAYE

That's my girl. She's always been a Tomboy, or rather was. That changed about two years ago when she started dating.

Points to a sports trophy or to a team photograph.

She played T-ball at first, then soccer. She was terrible at soccer, but she mastered tripping people without being caught. The other teams hated her, but our little crew cheered her on and booed the refs.

Laughs.

Poor guys, just trying to do their job in those silly, unflattering, shorts. Then it was softball and Track. Swimming for a bit, and martial arts. She never sat still.

JEFF

I never played anything. Except the violin. Dad made me until I was twelve. Then I broke the thing trying to whack a mouse that was running around the music room terrifying Mrs. Cleaver. Dang thing crawled into a Tuba and we couldn't get it out. We never told Ricky Wassermen. We just called him mouse blower.

FAYE

You're something else Jeff. Guess that's our generation's fault. We're all single parents with wild kids.

JEFF

Hey, we're not that wild. We don't start wars. We don't rape the planet for oil.

FAYE

We were hippies once too. Then we got old.

JEFF

How's that old song go, "Hope I die before I get old"?

FAYE

Yeah. The Who. They used to smash their guitars on stage. Pete and Roger are senior citizens now.

JEFF

Right.

So Mrs. Cooper, about Summer. Something happened between us.

FAYE

No kidding. You two have been whispering and sneaking around for weeks, and now nothing. Silence. And now you're breaking into my house. Whatever's going on with you two, it must be big.

But look, as long as the house doesn't burn down, whatever it is, it's Ok with me.

JEFF

I doubt that.

FAYE

Is it drugs?

JEFF

No.

FAYE

Then it's fine Jeff. I was a kid once too you know. I did my share of crazy and stupid things. I had a brother and we always fought. Now we call each other all time. It'll work out, whatever it is. Frankly I have other more important things on my mind right now. Mainly your father.

You know what he asked me right?

JEFF

Playing dumb.

No. What?

FAYE

He asked me to marry him.

JEFF

Oh. Um. Wow.

FAYE

Yes wow. And that would make Summer your sister. That's probably what she's upset about. It's not anything you did, she's not ready to be a sister and lose her precious spot as the center of my attention.

JEFF

Somehow, I don't think that's the problem, but oh man. My sister? That's just messed up.

FAYE

She's not really listening to Jeff.

Why would your father propose to me Jeff? Does he propose to a lot of people? I've got to know this.

JEFF

Nope, just mom. 'Course he did that twice.

FAYE

This can't be real. We barely know each other. We're in love yeah, but marriage? Is there something I should know Jeff? Is he sick? Bad heart? What? Why would he do this?

JEFF

Maybe it's the baby. Maybe he thinks it'll help.

Jeff starts to panic as he realizes what he's said.

FAYE

Baby? What baby? Oh. I get it. He must have found the test strip. Finally. That explains everything.

Doesn't he know how those things work? Silly man.

It's kind of sweet though. Kind of noble.

I admit I was kind of looking forward to it - the baby - a chance to play mom again. Do it right this time.

JEFF

Jeff can't figure out what Faye's talking about, but he's relieved she isn't yelling.

You're not mad?

FAYE

Mad? Why would I be mad? In fact this helps a lot. Thanks Jeff.

JEFF

Man. Mrs. C?

Shakes his head.

You make about as much sense as your daughter.

FAYE

Thanks Jeff. That means a lot.

END OF SCENE.

SCENE 3

> Dan's home, the living room. Same time as the last scene. Summer and Dan are sitting on the couch.

SUMMER

I don't know who else to talk to Mr. York. My mom won't listen, and Jeff is, well he's Jeff.

DAN

I know what exactly what you mean. Jeff drives me crazy sometimes, but he means well, deep down – and he does listen, it just takes him a long time to change. As for your mom, well, she's more of a doer than a listener.

> *Looks up to see Summer is impatiently waiting for him to finish.*

I'm sorry, you were saying?

SUMMER

It's about this marriage. It's for the wrong reasons. There's something you need to know.

DAN

> *Dan clutches his chest for dramatic emphasis.*

Oh god. She's going to turn me down isn't she! I blew it! Damn! Can't I do anything right? She's so perfect. So sweet. Funny. Smart. I can't lose her now. She's like a part of me. A part that's been missing for so long I didn't even know it was gone. And now if I lose it again, I'll know it. I'll always feel it. Never whole! Oh God.

> *Dan takes a deep breath.*

SUMMER

It's not like that. Yeah Mom's freaked out and all -

DAN

-Too fast. I went too fast. I always do that. Jump right to the end. Bottom line. Read the end of the book before I start the first page to make sure the story's worth reading. I screwed up the best thing that's ever happened to me. I won't get another chance. I'm such an idiot.

SUMMER

> *Yelling.*

Mr. York! It's not like that!

SUMMER

Normal voice.

The problem's not with mom. It's with me.

DAN

Oh! Honey? I'm so sorry. Blended marriages are so tough on kids. You're right. We should have waited until you were settled into college before yanking apart your life like this. What was I thinking -

SUMMER

Summer stands and stomps around.

-ARRGGH! What is it with men? ARRGGH!

DAN

I'm sorry honey. I'm just really on the edge. That's not an excuse, but that's how it is. I'll be quiet. Just tell me what it is. I promise not to interrupt.

SUMMER

Long beat.

I'm pregnant.

DAN

What?

SUMMER

I'm knocked up. Me. Not mom. You're marrying mom because you think she's having your baby, and you're wrong. I'm having the baby.

Beat.

You don't need to marry her.

DAN

Beat.

Dan stands up, his tone changes to lecturing.

Actually I do.

Before this. Before what you...

Dan runs his hands through his hair.

DAN

I wasn't sure if she'd keep the child. It's pretty risky at her age, but I wanted to be there for her no matter what. I thought about all that she must be going through, and I wanted to be there for her.

Thinking Faye was having our child just woke me to the fact that I would love to have a child with her. I woke up to the truth.

I really do love her.

SUMMER

I'm sorry. I didn't know.

Trying not to cry.

I didn't… I just didn't want anyone to hurt mom. Not like dad did. I don't want to see her like that - ever. I don't want that. I don't.

DAN

I won't hurt her Summer. Well, not anymore than the average couple that fights over stupid things like taking out the trash. I promise.

SUMMER

Dan offers to hug Summer, she lets him and starts crying. He holds her until she stops, and then he gently lets go.

You smell like Jeff - when he remembers to shower.

DAN

Same aftershave.

He spilled it all over himself on his first prom. Could've peeled the paint off the walls.

SUMMER

Jeff went to prom?

DAN

Yeah, surprised me too. Pretty girl. Jesse something. They dated for a few weeks then she cheated on him. He's never had a steady girl since.

SUMMER

Mr. York -

DAN

- Dan's fine.

SUMMER

Dan.

It's Jeff.

He's the father.

DAN

Crosses the room. Clearly upset

SUMMER

It just kind of happened. It's my fault. I wasn't taking my pills like I should. They make me feel all bloated and I hold water like a balloon, and I thought, I thought I had the days counted right -

DAN

- Last I heard it takes two people to make a baby.

SUMMER

I told him it was Ok, and we were out of condoms -

DAN

- Out? How often was this going on?

SUMMER

A lot. It was joke at first -

DAN

Yelling.

- Sex is not a joke!

SUMMER

That's not what I meant. I mean we weren't serious -

DAN

Yelling.

- It's serious now! This is as serious as it gets! Didn't the two of you learn anything from us? It's hell raising kids on your own! It screws up everything! Didn't you suffer enough growing up? Do you really want to do that to your own kid?

SUMMER

Runs out the front door in tears.

Summer exits.

DAN

Dan's reaction is frozen in shock at his own anger and the reaction. As the door slams shut he reacts like it struck him, and he staggers. He grips the couch arm for support. He gasps for breath. He starts to panic as he realizes he cannot catch he breath. He clutches his chest from shooting pain. He looks around lost and confused, the pain obvious. Then all at once he looks very ill, and faints. He falls to the ground in front of the couch, landing in a way not visible to from the front door.

FAYE

Arrives at the front door. She knocks at the door, waits, and knocks again. She tests the handle, and finds it open.

Faye enters.

Dan?

Faye is noticeably agitated as she crosses the room. She does not see Dan on the floor.

Are you home? The door wasn't locked.

She senses that something's wrong. She walks over to the hallway door and calls out loudly.

Dan?

Exits through door to inner house.

Talks off stage.

We need to talk. About the other night. I need to explain…Where are you?

Reenters.

Huh. Maybe he stepped out.

Looks outside, preferably a window.

Not taking out the trash.

Takes out her cell phone. Dials.

Dan's phone rings in the room.

FAYE

She looks around confused. Follows the sound around the couch and sees him. She screams and drops her phone. She goes to him and tries to check and see if he's OK, but she can't figure out how to check.

Dan, oh-my-god Dan!

She shakes him.

Wake up damn you! I don't know what to do! Help! Somebody Help!

She grabs his cell phone. She can't figure out how to dial it.

Why the hell do they make these things so damn hard to use!

She tosses it aside and runs over and finds her phone. She stares at it.

What the hell do I dial!

She hits herself in the head with palm of her hand.

Think damn it! Summer!

She dials.

Pick up! Damnit! Pick up, pick up, Pick up! Ahhh! It's an emergency! Call me when you get this!

Hangs up. She's visibly shaking. She dials again.

411. Hello? No. This is an emergency. I know, but this was all I could think of! You'll connect me? Thank god. Thank you, thank you, thank you! Hello? My husband's on the floor! I don't know! I found him like that when I came home! I don't know! How do I do that?

She goes back to him, checking his lips for breath, and his wrist for a pulse.

Yes he's breathing. His pulse - I can't find it! Yes I did that! Oh wait, it's there! It's there…

Crying now, she loosens the collar on his shirt.

Yes, it's 2700 Parklane. Brown house. Yes. I'll be here.

Lights go down.

END OF SCENE.

SCENE 4

> Faye's living room, just after the last scene. Summer and Jeff are sitting facing each other on the couch, and it's clear they've been arguing for awhile, and have reached a pause. Jeff breaks the silence between them.

JEFF

That's not him.

SUMMER

You weren't there. He was horrible.

JEFF

I didn't have to be there. He's my dad. I've heard it all before, and that wasn't him.

SUMMER

So I made it up, is that it? I'm just a lying bitch and a whore. Nice to know where I stand in you're family.

JEFF

Jeff rubs his forehead like he has a headache.

Summer…

SUMMER

Don't you patronize me! Don't you dare! I hate you! Both of you!

JEFF

Great way to raise our kid. Hating his family.

SUMMER

Stop saying that! He's mine!

JEFF

It's not going to work Summer. I'm not falling for it. I'm not fighting with you.

SUMMER

Cut the holier than thou crap Jeff! I was just another notch for you. Another toy to blog about. You've been bragged already? 'Hey I nailed my half sister! Woo hoo!'

JEFF

I've told one friend. And I said I was with a girl so great, she might be the one.

SUMMER

You're so full of shit your eyes are brown.

JEFF

Gets up and starts pacing to walk off his anger.

What's with you? How emo can a person get? All you are is 'Anger, anger, anger, and a moat of fury'.

SUMMER

That's not you talking.

JEFF

No. It's a quote from my dad in one of his books. He told me he was referring to mom.

Guess I've got one of those Edible complexes.

SUMMER

It's Oedipus. And you're kinda using it wrong, but I get your point. You're mom was a jerk, so you're attracted to jerks like me.

JEFF

Stops pacing.

No. I meant … No that's more or less what I meant. Except for the jerk part.

Awkward pause.

My dad might have been mad, but he doesn't hate you. He doesn't hate anybody. He doesn't know how. He puts on the news and bitches about Bush then makes apologies for him in the same breath.

SUMMER

Mom will kick me out. I know it. I'll have to get some crappy job that doesn't pay shit. Or two.

JEFF

You're mom takes in stray goldfish from her coworkers. She won't kick you out.

SUMMER

You really do pay attention to things. Even when you're all spacey and stoned looking, you really are listening aren't you?

JEFF

Yeah. I'm thinking of getting a degree in Psychology.

Summer laughs.

No joke. I don't know what I want to do - nothing really - but everywhere you go there's people. Can't hurt to know how they work.

SUMMER

I don't know what I want either. Mom thinks I'm going to be some kind of engineer, but I'm thinking of Journalism, or maybe a Veterinarian.

JEFF

You do know that loud voices startle animals?

SUMMER

Sarcastically.

Ha ha.

JEFF

I thought you had all of these plans for college? I thought you got in? Don't you have to know what you're doing?

SUMMER

Nah. That's just the game you've got to play. Everybody changes their majors.

JEFF

I considered the Navy. Dad threw a fit, but then said he'd support me. Then I went out on my bud's boat for party and puked for a week from the swaying. So much for that.

SUMMER

You do know how to lie. As long as it's to make someone smile.

JEFF

Something will work out. Just stop fighting the world long enough to give it a chance. That's not a quote. That's just how I get by.

SUMMER

Her cell phone rings. She looks at it.

Mom again. Can't she let me be.

She ignores the ringing, no intention of answering it.

JEFF

His phone rings. He checks it.

It's your mom.

SUMMER

Don't answer that. I'm not ready for her. I know she talked to your dad.

JEFF

Answers it. Summer makes angry gestures while he talks.

Yeah. She's here. Your house. Where? What? Oh man. Yeah. Five to ten minutes? Room 203? Yeah. Thanks.

He gets up and makes motions to leave, checking for keys, etc.

SUMMER

What?

JEFF

Dad's in the cardiac unit at County General.

Lights down on Summer's reaction.

END OF SCENE.

SCENE 5

> A few hour later, in the waiting area of a Hospital emergency room. Summer is seated, Faye is pacing.

FAYE

They let me ride in the ambulance, why won't they let me in the room! Why won't they tell me what's going on! I told them we were engaged! I have a ring! I know the shape of his appendix scar! This is so damn stupid!

> *Faye yells at an unseen nurse.*

You can take your HIPA bullshit and stuff it up your –

SUMMER

- MOM! You'll get us thrown out! Then what?

FAYE

I hate this. It's been hours! They took him away with all of these tubes sticking out of him; he looked so pale, like they were sucking away his life with each damn beep of the machine. And machines fail - all the time! That's what I do! I fix stupid machines - and those stupid doctors are trusting Dan's life to a stupid machine and the stupid nurses won't let me see him because this whole damn place is STUPID!

> *Faye breathes heavily and slowly, trying to get back in control.*

SUMMER

At least Jeff is with him. He'll tell us what's going on.

FAYE

Really? Unless he needs money for a vending machine we won't be seeing him.

SUMMER

Mom!

FAYE

Jeff had an F and a pair of D's on his midterms. His father's a professor. How do you think that makes Dan feel? Like dirt. Jeff doesn't care. The only things I've ever seen Jeff give a damn about is beer, sleeping, and microwave pizza.

SUMMER

Stop it! Stop it! STOP IT!

> *Gathers herself for a beat.*

Don't take this out on Jeff. Don't.

FAYE

Faye seems about to argue but looks at Summer and relents.

I'm sorry.

Faye makes a visible effort to calm down before continuing.

I just can't deal with this. I was so used to being on my own. I had it all under control. All I had to worry about was you and me, and you were the perfect child. You're grades were great, you helped out with the housework, you obeyed every rule, and you were there for me when all we had was that rat hole apartment and that damn Ford.

And then Dan has to come along and rip that all away. No time to adjust. No long term plans. No getting to know each other. He just walks in and fits. It's just not fair. He fit so damn well that now all I have is a hole where he's supposed to be. I don't need that. I don't want it. I had that hole all boarded up! I was OK.

I just can't go through this again. I can't. I can't be alone again.

He has to be Ok. And I have to KNOW he's Ok.

And if he's not... I don't know what to do.

I hate being in love. I hate it. With all my damn heart I HATE it!

SUMMER

No, no, no. Not you too. I didn't know, I swear. I didn't think it was like that. I just thought...

FAYE

What are you talking about?

SUMMER

I wasn't ready.

FAYE

Ready? Ready for what?

SUMMER

To move on. To move away. To move out of our home. To go away to school. To change! I wasn't ready.

FAYE

None of us are.

Mother birds have to shove their chicks out of the nest - because no one ever wants to leave home.

SUMMER

Mom. This is my fault.

FAYE

Darling, of 'course it's not your fault.

SUMMER

It is. We had a fight. Just before this happened. We are arguing - and I ran off.

FAYE

You and Dan. Were arguing? And you ran off! What about? What were you arguing about?

SUMMER

Crying.

He was fine when I left. He was upset, but he was fine. I didn't know this would happen! It's all my fault! I ruin everything I touch!

FAYE

Faye instinctively moves to comfort her, but Summer backs away.

Arguments happen dear. It's not your fault.

SUMMER

Yes it is. God! Why don't you ever listen to me.

FAYE

Fine. I'm listening now. Just tell me.

SUMMER

I told him…

I told him I slept with Jeff. I did it to make him mad, to make you mad. To drive you apart!

FAYE

Oh Summer, honey, this isn't your fault, it's mine. I should have been there for you! I was so worried about how this was affecting me, that I ignored you. It's only natural you acted out and -

SUMMER

- MOTHER! For once in your LIFE - listen to me! Let me finish!

FAYE

Faye steels herself because she does not normally let anyone talk to her this way.

Go on.

SUMMER

I'm pregnant. It's Jeff's. The playing around got serious, and I couldn't help myself. I don't even like him. Not really. He can be sweet - and a jerk - but he's got something... no... he was just there. Just...there.

I wanted to yell at you. Tell you to stay home - with me - but he was the one that was there. That's all it was.

Faye starts to talk, but Summer glares her into silence.

I know what you're going to say. It's stupid. I know it's stupid. But it's what you did with daddy! You got pregnant, so you married him. And I swore I'd never let that happen to me and now...now it's too late. I'm you.

FAYE

I don't know what to say.

SUMMER

Yell at me. Tell me I'm an idiot. That's what Dan did. That's why he's here. I took the only thing good that ever happened to you AND I RUINED IT!

Summer falls apart.

FAYE

Faye's anger disappears when she sees her daughter hurting. She wraps Summer in her arms, and holds her until she stops crying.

It took me a long time to forgive myself. I hated my life - every day, every minute. I dragged myself to night school. I dragged myself to work. I clenched my teeth and bit my tongue every time I spoke to a boss. And I put that all away, every time - when I looked at you. You were the one thing I did right. You made it all worthwhile.

Wipes her daughters tears, brushes back her hair.

You didn't ruin anything.

SUMMER

How can you say that?

FAYE

Who was the one who talked me into dating again, huh? Who was the one who made me pick up the phone when Dan called the next day? Who was there for me? You were.

If it weren't for you, there wouldn't be anything to ruin.

SUMMER

You're insane mom.

FAYE

Maybe. If so, I raised a crazy daughter.

SUMMER

I'm SO sorry mom.

FAYE

I know. So was I.

And I don't think you know this, but my mother went to her grave not forgiving me. I shamed her. I didn't do the things she wanted me to do.

She shut me out. Completely. That's not going to happen to us.

No matter what you do, you are my daughter, and I will ALWAYS forgive you.

Lights down.

END OF SCENE

SCENE 6

Same time as the last scene. A hospital emergency room with a single hospital bed. Dan is hooked up to machines that beep quietly, he is asleep. Jeff is sitting slumped in a chair watching him.

JEFF

Sits up a little.

You know, I hate seeing you like this. And I don't know if you can hear me, but you need to come back. You need to be here. This is not...It's not right. You're the one who's good with things. You always know what to do. I don't. I can't do this on my own. I don't want to do it on my own.

No. That's selfish. I don't just need you here, I want you here. I'll even let you lecture me. For three hours - and I won't argue, or talk back.

DAN

Voice raspy.

I'll need four hours. You were really a bad kid this time.

JEFF

Stands up and goes to the bedside, not quite believing Dan is awake.

You're alright? Do I need to get the Nurse? What thing do I push? They told me to push something and I don't remember what it was!

DAN

Dan has trouble speaking, it's tough for him to catch his breath. He's tired, and struggling to seem well.

Good thing I'm not dying then.

I don't want to be in the obituaries because my son couldn't follow instructions.

My luck, there will be a teacher's lounge in purgatory, and I'll be stuck there, never hearing the end of it.

JEFF

Does it hurt? Can I do anything?

DAN

You could take the invisible elephant off my chest.

JEFF

Dad -

DAN

- I was having a lot of odd dreams. It's hard to figure out what happened, and what didn't.

I hope the sponge bath was real.

I think I dreamed up the nurse's outfit though -

JEFF

-    Quit it.

You're just trying to make me laugh. You do that when you don't want to tell me something.

DAN

Look.

I don't know how I am, or how I'm going to be.

I woke up earlier and they told me a bunch of things and I don't remember them, but I don't think it was anything bad.

I remember reassurance. I think.

Did they tell you anything?

JEFF

A bunch of stuff I didn't understand.

DAN

Like father, like son.

JEFF

Yeah. In a lot of ways.

Long beat.

So what happened? Is this about me? Me and Summer I mean.

DAN

Dan finds his strength, and grows more confident and assured as he speaks.

No. It's about life. And how it just goes along in a boring routine, and then one day smacks you in the knees with a 2 by 4. No matter how prepared you are, life always has a better offense.

To tell the truth, I thought I was dead. I had this thing down my throat, and another out my, well you know, down there, and I felt like my body had gotten a dozen times heavier. Nothing worked on its own. I tried to move and couldn't. I tried to pee and couldn't. I tried to breathe and nothing happened. It was like being buried alive. I thought, this is it - I'm stuck like this forever.

So I started praying. To myself mostly. Promising my body that if it started working again, I'd do things different. When nothing happened I prayed to God, to anyone, just to let me try again. Then the Doctors and nurses came, and it felt like a miracle, like I'd been released. Then they yanked that thing out of my throat and I could breathe again and talk, and I swear I've never felt so alive.

They asked me a million questions, but none of them asked what I'd do different, and then I knew - it wasn't a miracle. This was routine for them. I was just another body. Nothing special had happened. I was just alive, and this is just another day.

But now that I'm talking to you, I know that something has changed. I'm not the same. I want to live. I don't think I ever felt that way before. I was just getting through the day, doing what I need to do, existing, but not living.

I want you to do me a favor.

JEFF

What.

DAN

I want to talk to Faye. Alone. Then all of you.

JEFF

Ok.

DAN

Do you mind? I know this has got to be hell on you too. But there's something I have to do.

JEFF

I guess.

> *Jeff turns to walk away, but stops and turns back.*

Dad?

> *Jeff almost can't say it.*

I love you.

DAN

I love you too.

And I don't think you've said that… since you were… six.

It's good to hear.

Let's not wait another 12 years before saying it again.

Lights down.

END OF SCENE

SCENE 7

>An hour later, same setting as the last scene. Dan is still
>hooked up to the machines, but he's awake. Faye is on
>one side holding his hand. They are talking quietly and
>stop when then the children come in.
>Jeff and Summer walk in just after the lights go up.

DAN

Sits up a little.

I think this is the scene where I'm supposed to tell you who's inheriting my Kingdom.

FAYE

Not funny Dan. You'll scare them.

It's a case of Angina, and he fainted from it, but he's Ok. No stroke, no clot, no concussion, but they're keeping him for observations just to be sure -

DAN

- Apparently I've been having minor attacks for a while. Stiffness, numb shoulder, but I didn't realize what it was. I put it down to being old -

FAYE

- It's taken a turn for the worse, but he's on blood thinners, and he needs to cut out some of the junk he eats - but the Doctor says he's fairly healthy, for someone who doesn't exercise regularly -

DAN

- You're just happy that you have someone to drag you to the gym now.

SUMMER

Summer moves closer to the bed to get they're attention.

I need to, I mean, I... I'm sorry -

DAN

- Stop. We're past the point of blame. We're all at fault here. Don't put this all on your shoulders. I know acting out when I see it. Well in hindsight anyways. We are where we are. We need to move on.

FAYE

No.

There's something that still bothers me.

FAYE

To Summer.

I want to know WHAT you were doing talking to DAN before coming to ME?

JEFF

Summer starts to argue, but Jeff steps up and touches her, and she quiets down. He speaks up instead.

She tried. I tried. You weren't listening.

FAYE

Faye starts to talk, but Dan clutches her hand with both of his. Instead of arguing, she covers her mouth with her hand.

DAN

It's over.

You're mother and I talked about it. About a lot of things.

First, we're getting married. For no reason other than we like each other.

But there's a second. We'd like to adopt your child.

When you're on your feet, we'll give you back custody, or we can continue to raise the child as our own. Either way is fine with us.

SUMMER

I don't know what to say.

FAYE

You don't have to say yes. It's an offer. Take it or leave it. If you leave it? It stays open - if you change your mind down the road.

DAN

But we're serious about the custody.

If we're the parents, we want to be the parents. No arguing about the little things.

FAYE

And we DO want to be parents. Again. Enough that if you say no, we may adopt anyways, but it's not going to be easy at our age, and Dan's health...

JEFF

What's he going to call me? Dad or Bro?

SUMMER

Jeff -

JEFF

- It's a real question. People talk. It would be weird.

SUMMER

We need to think about it.

JEFF

We? There's a 'we' now?

SUMMER

We. For now anyways. I don't know about tomorrow, but for right now, there's a we.

JEFF

Jeff let's go of Summer.

Wow. Um, I don't know if there is a smart way to tell you this, but I don't know. This is WAY too much deal with in one day. I need -

DAN

- Take your time. It may not look like it...

Waves his arm with tubes hanging off of him.

But we're not going anywhere.

SUMMER

Summer is finally all alone, she loses it.

I didn't mean for all this to happen!

DAN

Nobody means for stuff like this to happen. It just does. That's just life.

It's not how we screw up our lives that matters - it's what we do about it afterwards - that's what matters.

FAYE

To Summer.

I will say that this was the dumbest idea you've ever had, and that's saying a lot.

But I think you were protecting me - in your own weird way. Or rebelling. Or just being a teenager. I don't care.

We'll get by. We always have. Always will.

DAN

And I'm done dating and marrying people. Faye's the end of that. I'm quitting while I'm ahead.

So Jeff... If you and Summer break up?

You'll have to start dating outside of the family.

JEFF

Dad, you are so not funny.

Lights down.

THE END

Settling

This was my first submission to the ten-minute play festival. I hadn't tried writing a play in several years, and had been living in Yellow Springs for only a year. I met several local actors and they all knew I'd written plays and comics. They urged me to submit something, so I did.

I found 10 minutes extremely complicated to write for. It's long enough for a scene, but not long enough for a big set up or climax. I went through several ideas over a year and completed a few plays that I rejected as just not right. The idea for this play, *Settling* came to me at the last minute. I blitzed through the script and the revisions in one month in order to submit it on time.

It was accepted and produced in a strange but clever way. I'll explain it, but it will make more sense after you read the play:

A table and two chairs was set up at the beginning of the festival, off to the side of the stage on riser, and off to the side from the audience. Unannounced, an actor was seated by a waiter, and the waiter left as the festival started. The actor sat there, looking bored and killing time for the entire first set of plays. Nearly an hour. After intermission he returned to his spot and when the lights came on, it wasn't to the main stage, it was to the side stage and the play began. The production was elegantly acted and directed. Enough to convince me I needed to do this again.

CHARACTERS

Ryan	A man in his early 40s.
Anne	A woman in her early 40s

TIME

Early evening. The present.

SETTING

Nice restaurant. We only need to see one table setting for two. There are two identical place settings. One place setting is unoccupied. Folded Napkin, filled wine glass. There are two menus on the table.

ACT I

SCENE 1

> AT RISE:
> RYAN is seated at the table. He's dressed for a nice night out. He's waiting for ANNE who is late and nervously tapping his feet.

ANNE

Enters rushing. Dressed in clothes far too casual for a date, like sweats or torn jeans.

So sorry. Between traffic and parking I nearly gave up.

Picks up the glass of wine.

Is this mine, Ryan?

She downs it quickly as Ryan nods. Then she sits down heavily and sprawls out, relaxed.

I needed that. Can we do another? Who's our waiter?

RYAN

I'm not sure anymore. It's been so long I think they changed shifts.

ANNE

Really? Then why didn't you eat? You didn't have to wait for me.

RYAN

I was trying to be polite, Anne.

ANNE

Starving isn't polite. It's stupid. Did you at least order appetizers?

RYAN

No. I couldn't make up my mind.

ANNE

Picks up her menu, scans over it.

Imagine that. Ryan not making up his mind. How about nachos? Nobody can screw up nachos.

RYAN

Anything you want is fine with me.

ANNE

Eye's him with apprehension.

Since when are you agreeable and not picky? What happened? Is it my birthday? Did someone die?

RYAN

Nobody died.

ANNE

Are you sure? It's a big world. I'm sure somebody somewhere out there died.

RYAN

Nobody I know died.

ANNE

Then what's up? We never agree on food. I eat everything, while you hate everything. It's our thing.

RYAN

I don't hate everything.

ANNE

Fine. I'll play along.

Looks at the menu again.

Parmesan Brussel sprouts. That's what we're having.

RYAN

Ok. That I hate. No cabbage golf balls.

ANNE

Jalapeño poppers?

RYAN

You know spicy food doesn't agree with me.

ANNE

Indeed I do. I can also do this all day. Fried Calamari? Crunchy and chewy.
Wriggles down your throat.

RYAN

Nachos are fine.

ANNE

Puts menu aside.

Hah. Decision made. I knew you could do it. So why did you invite me out? It's not
our movie night this month.

RYAN

No reason. I wanted to go out.

ANNE

Really? Nothing to do with my divorce then?

RYAN

No.

ANNE

Because it's final. As of today. Signed, sealed and thank the maker it's over.

RYAN

Just a coincidence.

ANNE

Pokes at table for emphasis.

I smell smoke. Something's on fire. It's not the kitchen. Must be your pants, liar.

RYAN

*Pauses to sigh and compose himself. Nothing is going as he
imagined.*

You're right. I'm lying.

ANNE

No kidding. Your eyebrows always twitch when you're lying. It's your tell.

RYAN

Touches his eyebrows absently.

I do not have a tell.

ANNE

Let's agree to disagree. Because you do.

RYAN

LOUDLY.

Fine. I do. I have a tell. And I'm a liar. *Thanks* for pointing it out.

ANNE

Suddenly concerned.

What's wrong?

RYAN

Nothing's wrong.

ANNE

Ryan. What's wrong?

She reaches across the table and takes his hand in hers.

RYAN

This is your third divorce. And it's my second.

ANNE

No. That's not how it works. Jan left you. And Marla cheated on you. Those were not your fault.

RYAN

Doesn't matter who's fault it is.

ANNE

Of course it does. I left Jeremy because he was boring. Chad and I had nothing in common other than sex. Larry, well Larry's Larry. Neither of us know why I married Larry.

RYAN

You said it was for security. For his money.

ANNE

But I'm not getting any of it. So fat lot of good that did me. My point is, I like to crash and burn. I accept that about me. You, on the other hand, are far too dedicated to idiots that don't deserve you. So unlike me, your divorces don't count. You were the good guy. You tried to make them work. You just need to find someone who's worth your effort.

RYAN

Takes a long beat. Composing his thoughts. ANNE waits impatiently.

Remember when we were in high school?

ANNE

Depends. Are we talking classes or parties? There are several parties I do not remember.

RYAN

Germany. The bus tour we went on for language class?

ANNE

You mean the stifling hot thing with no AC? The thing we had to raise money for all spring only to hate every second of?

RYAN

Yeah that one.

ANNE

Nope. Blotted out of memory. Forgotten along with my 80s hair.

RYAN

You really forgot?

ANNE

Is there a point to this? Because I'm not seeing one.

RYAN

The promise. The one we made? The one about when we turned thirty?

ANNE

Thinking. Not recalling. Then it comes up.

Oh… That.

RYAN

Yeah. That.

ANNE

You're serious?

RYAN

Sort of. Why not?

ANNE

Because we were stupid kids sneaking beer.

RYAN

We each said if we don't find Mr. or Mrs. Right before we're thirty, we'd settle for marrying each other.

ANNE

We're both in our forties. Statute of limitations ran out.

RYAN

So what. We've known each other since junior high. We've never stopped hanging out. We've been there for each other when no one else was.

ANNE

We tried this. It didn't work.

RYAN

One drunk night of sex doesn't define a relationship.

ANNE

I dunno. It was pretty bad.

RYAN

It wasn't that bad.

ANNE

It was so bad we vowed to never bring it up.

RYAN

Well I'm bringing it up.

ANNE

Two raccoons fighting over a trash can have more chemistry then we do.

RYAN

RYAN pounds the table in frustration.

So fine. We don't have sex. We just share a place together.

ANNE

Looks around to see if anyone is paying attention to them.

You're serious.

RYAN

At what point in this conversation did you think I wasn't serious? I'm just tired of being alone.

ANNE

I get that. But it's been two years since Marla. Just Move on.

RYAN

I've tried. I can barely text on my phone, but now I have to swipe? I don't get it. Dating is horrible.

ANNE

Yeah it is. Why do you think I said yes to Larry?

RYAN

If you can settle for Larry, why don't you settle for me?

ANNE

You *are* serious.

RYAN

We've been over this. Yes, I'm serious! Everyone I've ever met has been a huge compromise. If I'm going to settle for someone, why not settle for someone I already like and get along with?

ANNE

I didn't know you felt this way.

RYAN

We screwed in a park during your family's picnic!

ANNE

It was that or potato sack races! Potatoes!

RYAN

Fine. It was a dumb idea. Forget I ever brought this up.

RYAN looks at the menu. Avoids any eye contact.

ANNE

Beat.

It wasn't a dumb idea. You just surprised me.

RYAN

Fish. I think I'll get the fish.

ANNE

You hate the smell of fish.

RYAN

This is made with lemons and capers. That will cover up anything. I'm getting the fish.

ANNE

I just got divorced. What did you expect me to say?

RYAN

You should get the lamb. There's a mint sauce. You like mint.

ANNE

Stop this. Just talk to me.

RYAN

There's nothing to say. You don't want to settle, and I do. Perfectly understandable. You're attractive. You're in your prime. Why should *you* stop looking?

ANNE

What about you? You're responsible. You can cook. You remember birthdays. You refuse to be in debt. You're USDA choice prime beef compared to most guys. You could have anyone woman you want.

RYAN

Says the woman turning me down.

ANNE

Why are you so set on this?

RYAN

Doesn't matter. Pick out something. We'll eat. See a crappy movie and go home.

ANNE

Can we make fun of the movie?

RYAN

What's the point in a crappy movie if we can't make fun of it?

ANNE

Thinks for a beat.

It would be nice to not come home to an empty house.

RYAN

I've lived alone for two years. You'll get used to it.

ANNE

I don't sleep well unless someone is next to me.

RYAN

You snore like a lawn mower running out of gas.

ANNE

I know! Well I don't know. I'm asleep. But everybody tells me that. Why would you want that?

RYAN

I wouldn't. I'm a light sleeper.

ANNE

I roll in bed. Over and over. Back and forth. Wrap myself in the sheets. Makes everyone freeze.

RYAN

Beat.

So why don't we try six months. If it fails? It fails. If it works? We try another six.
Then we go on from there.

ANNE

Beat.

I have three more months on my lease.

RYAN

So keep it. I only have two rooms. I don't have enough place for all the junk you
collect.

ANNE

I have three rooms. You could have one, and I could have one.

RYAN

I don't want to sleep alone anymore. If you don't want to do this, that's fine.
Really.

ANNE

Maybe I'm just scared. You ever think of that?

RYAN

And I'm not?

ANNE

We have a good thing. Why ruin it?

RYAN

Ruin what? We've survived almost thirty years as friends. Neither Jan nor Marla
ever accepted that, you and me. They hated it. Both thought we were secretly
cheating.

ANNE

You think my guys were any better? Chad hated all the nerd shit we would talk
about. Larry thought you were gay, so he didn't care. Jeremy would go through my
phone texts. He was so pissed to find out we weren't cheating that he accused me of
deleting all the good stuff.

RYAN

Maybe they all knew something we didn't.

ANNE

If you lived with me, you'd end up hating me. And if you gave up on me, then I'd have nothing. I can't deal with that!

RYAN

You made your point. Living together is a mistake.

ANNE

I didn't say that. Sex is a mistake.

RYAN

So we don't sleep together. Just next to each other. You can date other people. Just come home to me.

ANNE

You don't mean that. Nobody could mean that.

RYAN

I mean it. I've gone two years without sex. I doubt any of the parts still work.

ANNE

You're serious.

RYAN

No. I'm kidding.

Why on earth would I want to spend any more time with you than I already do?

ANNE

Because I'm awesome?

RYAN

Glad *neither* of us is being serious.

Awkward silence.

ANNE

Doesn't this damn place have any waiters? I'm so hungry I'm going to gnaw my arm off.

RYAN

Let's just call it a night. I call you next week. That's our regular week. We'll do bad movie night then.

ANNE

I just want to make sure we know each other for thirty more years. I ruin every relationship. I don't want to ruin us.

RYAN

You haven't ruined us.

ANNE

Ponders.

Six months? ..Just to try it out?

RYAN

Six months.

ANNE

We'd get a better rate on a brand new place if we committed to twelve months.

RYAN

We could *definitely* afford several rooms if we combined our incomes.

ANNE

We'd only need one bedroom though... The rest could be storage…

RYAN

Or you could learn to throw things away?

ANNE

Don't hold your breath.

RYAN

I'm willing to do twelve months. No issues if it doesn't work. We stay friends.

ANNE

We stay friends.

RYAN

Beat.

We should try sex again. At least once.

Maybe we learned a thing or two after all of those marriages?

ANNE

Beat.

Or twice. Once could be a fluke. We won't know unless we try a few times.

Both look at each other like they want to do it right there and then on the table.

RYAN & ANNE

Waiter! Check!

BLACKOUT

END.

Thinly Veiled Reference

I wanted to write a farce, something that parodied the politics going on at the time. Politics are tough to tackle, and farce is difficult to reign in. I went through many drafts of this play, each time the satire getting more biting and broad to include both the left and the right. Being a satire, I got away with stereotypes and viewer knowledge to add more than I could fit on a page.

I wasn't sure this play would get accepted as it was a bit incendiary given the election that was ongoing at the time. It was also a bit more elaborate than some of the produced plays.

It was accepted and produced and fortunately got laughs in all the right places.

CHARACTERS

TED	Male. Hipster. Man bun, fedora, or long beard. 20-30s.
ALICE	Female. Soccer-mom. 30-40s.
CAROL	Androgynous. Vegan. Dread locks. Late teen to 20s.
BOB	Male. Average guy. 60s.

NOTE: All are dressed in pajamas for bedtime.

TIME

Middle of the Night. 2020.

SETTING

Kitchen in a suburban Midwest home. Stair case or entranceway to bedrooms, stage left. Window, table, four chairs stage left. Living room entrance, stage right of back wall. We can see through it the entrance, but only see black. EFX of smoke and fire will be the only things visible through doorway. At this point, only smoke. The smoke alarm is painted bright orange, and underneath it is a sign or writing that clearly reads "2020 Election". There are cabinets with a landline telephone on it. There's a cupboard with a prop fire extinguisher, and squirt bottle inside.

ACT I

SCENE 1

> Dark kitchen. Smoke alarm goes off loudly in the kitchen. Red light flashing.

BOB

Enters from bedrooms. Flicks light switch. Staring at smoke alarm. Half awake.

Lights up.

Looking at the alarm like he'd never seen a smoke alarm before.

TED

Enters from bedrooms. Walks over to the alarm in front of Bob. Takes the alarm of the wall, removes batteries.

Noise stops.

BOB

What are you doing!

TED

No emergency here, Bob. I'm Fixing the problem. Go back to bed.

BOB

But, that didn't solve anything Ted!

TED

Bob, stop being *SO* alarmist. This thing goes off all the time.

BOB

Ted. It's. A. Fire. Alarm. That's the perfect time to be an alarmist! It means our house is on FIRE!

TED

Allegedly. I haven't seen any fire. Have you?

BOB

No, but that doesn't mean it's not real!

TED

It's not affecting me personally, so I'm not concerned.

Alice and Carol enter from bedrooms. Sleepy.

CAROL

Why is everybody yelling?

BOB

The house is on fire, Carol!

TED

Allegedly.

BOB

A smoke alarm went off. Where there's smoke, there's fire.

CAROL

Are you sure? You paid for that noisy thing. Maybe you just want there to be a fire to justify it. For that matter, I don't even hear your "so called" smoke alarm.

She makes air quotes.

BOB

Pointing at Ted.

That's because Ted turned it off!

ALICE

You know... I had an alarm go off once... *So* annoying. I just hit the snooze button and went back to sleep. A few minutes later, *it was back.*

BOB

Alice... That's...

Thinks of the words.

False equivalency. Not EVERY alarm is the same. And *this* one is important!

TED

I just don't buy it Bob. I was reading online that smoking can be harmless when done in moderation. It can take years to do any long term damage.

ALICE

Yeah. I vape all the time. Smoke doesn't bother me.

BOB

Gah! *False. Equivalency*. Vaping isn't smoking. Smoking isn't a fire. This is a fire. *THIS* requires action.

TED

Fine. What kind of action? I'm *very* active in local demonstrations.

BOB

Demonstrations? What's that going to do? We need to act!

TED

There you go. Crushing my right to free speech and freedom to assemble. First amendment man.

BOB

I'm not telling you to – *argh*! Look. Would anyone else in the whole world *protest a fire*? No!

CAROL

You can't worry about the whole world, Bob. The truth is, all problems are local, and you know it.

BOB

Yes, I know, but this *IS* local, Carol. It's *our* house on fire.

CAROL

Good, I'm glad we can agree on the bigger picture. So then let's work the local issues. Like the newspapers.

BOB

Newspapers? Huh?

Confused

You mean, like, getting the press to investigate?

CAROL

Nooooo. I'm saying we have a lot of old newspapers. They're a fire hazard. We should *recycle* them.

ALICE

Oh, that's a wonderful idea! I'm *very* pro-environment. We always need to consider the environment, no matter what the problem is.

BOB

The environment isn't the issue! The newspapers don't matter right now!

ALICE

Dismissing Bob.

Bob, It is *never* too late to consider the environmental agenda.

TED

Cool beans. *Now* we're on a solid progressive agenda.

BOB

Alice, all of that *old* news is irrelevant!

CAROL

Oh *no*! You ignore the fourth estate at your own peril. Ask Nixon. I personally listen to NPR every day. We need in depth coverage, not alarmist sound bites. We need to do our research, understand our options, and carefully determine the reasons behind how we got here. That takes time and careful analysis.

BOB

Throws his hands up in the air in frustration.

It's too late to start that now! Last year? Sure. But the house is on fire *NOW*.

TED

Really bob? I've seen a lot of memes about how useless that old thing is, on social media.

Points to the alarm.

I'm very hesitant to support it.

Fire EFX seen in doorway. A red flickering light is good enough.

BOB

I'm done with you people. I'm getting the reliable fire extinguisher out of storage.

TED

Really? For one Bob, that brand has been tried before. It's just relying on name recognition. We just can't risk it.

BOB

Bob takes a fire extinguisher out of the cupboard and dusts it off.

Ted, why would you withhold your support for a well-known option?

Reading the instructions on the fire extinguisher

1) Look for obvious problem.

2) Point at obvious problem.

3) Shake hand vigorously and pull trigger.

4) Wait for results.

Shakes the extinguisher while looking in Ted's direction.

I've been loyal to this brand for a long time. It's consistent. It does what it says it will do. We have no reason not to try it.

TED

If I may. I have an alternative proposal.

BOB

Seriously? Like what?

TED

I make my own fire extinguishers. I've found that craft brewing is always superior to *commercial* efforts.

Ted goes into the same cupboard and takes out a common spray bottle.

BOB

That is just a water bottle.

TED

It's artisanal.

ALICE

Oooo. Can I see it? I love home grown solutions.

BOB

We don't have time to wait around!

>*Takes the fire extinguisher. Pulls the pin. Points. Nothing happens.*

TED

Called it.

TED

>*Sprays the fire with the bottle. Beat while they all stare and wait. Nothing happens.*

We need to give it a longer chance to effect change.

Fire EFX gets brighter.

BOB

Happy? We tried your way.

Enough with the *popular* solutions. I'm switching to *proven* leaders. I'm calling in the fire department. Let the *establishment* machine handle it.

CAROL

Wait, is *Joe* still the Fire Chief?

BOB

He's been in office *forever*, Carol. So, I assume so.

CAROL

Well that doesn't work for me. I heard his brother fired an inspector. What kind of honest man prevents inspectors from doing their job? Sounds pretty corrupt to me. What's he going to do when he's supposed to be fighting for us?

BOB

I don't know, maybe put out the fire like every other chief before him? Personally, I don't care WHAT his brother did or didn't do! Guy could beat hobos with a hockey stick for all I care! Just as long as he deals with *my* concerns.

CAROL

Oh Bob. Bob. I can't believe you said that. I had no idea you were hobo-phobic.

ALICE

Oh, those poor hobos. You know, I'm a vegan, so I know all about repressed cultures.

CAROL

Hobo-phobia is so rampant now a days. Hobos are simply terrified to come out of their boxcars. We, as a people, need to be more inclusive. I mean I'm not a hobo, but I do have friends that have experimented with being a hobo. I'm an ally, I fully support the hobo lifestyle.

ALICE

So brave Carol! I'm changing my fakebook profile right now to a rainbow bindle.

Takes out phone and starts typing

CAROL

Good idea! Me too!

Takes out phone and starts typing.

TED

Ted nods enthusiastically and does the same.

BOB

Look, I'm not opposed to the hobo agenda, but that's not our major concern right now.

ALICE

Ok, *Boomer*.

Alice waves dismissively.

BOB

Looks enraged at being called a boomer.

I'm Gen X thank you.

CAROL

If we had a woman as fire chief before now, we wouldn't be having this discussion.

TED

I hear you Carol, a woman ran for the job last time, but we didn't elect her. I don't think we're ready for female fire chiefs yet.

ALICE

Typical misogyny.

CAROL

You said it sister. I'm tired of this caveman attitude. A man just can't relate to how a fire will affect me, personally.

BOB

Fires affect everyone the same way. We all get burned.

ALICE

I'm just saying if we had a woman in charge, maybe we wouldn't GET burned.

Alice and Carol high five each other.

BOB

Fine. Next time a lady runs, I'll vote for her. Until then, lets support the fire man -

CAROL

Fire *Person.*

BOB

- Fire PERSON, that we have.

ALICE

Really Bob? How are women supposed to get fire experience if we don't use them. We won't ever shatter the glass ceiling that way.

BOB

I said next time.

He points up.

That's the only ceiling I'm worried about.

CAROL

It's always "next time" with you. I bet you don't even see your own privilege do you?

BOB

What does privilege have to do with this?

TED

Privilege is always at play. Have you seen the statistics on response times? White upper class neighborhoods get problems dealt with fast while the poor and people of color have to wait and end up burned again and again.

BOB

Well it's a good thing we're in a gentrified white neighborhood now, isn't it?

Dials phone. An old phone with a cord would be ideal, where Bob paces and gets tangled in the cord over the course of the scene.

Hold music starts playing

BOB

They put me on hold!

TED

I think we should just move to Canada. No fires up there.

CAROL

If we moved to a big fire state like California, we wouldn't have to worry about *these* kind of fires.

ALICE

Face buried in her phone.

There's pix of our house burning on Instagramma. Now it's on Flitter. I'm so going to make a meme of us. It's gonna get so *many* shares.

BOB

Panic setting in.

We're gonna die aren't we? We can't agree on anything. The fire is gonna win. That's how it all ends isn't it?

CAROL

What do you expect with men in charge?

TED

It's your generations fault. You created all this mess.

BOB

I'm not a boomer!

ALICE

Did I mention I'm a vegan?

Lights out. Fire still burning.

Coffee Time

There was a break in the festival productions for Covid, and was followed by a themed festival to tackle the issues that marginalized groups have struggled with. The following year though, I was itching to write something new. There's a strange magic to hearing actors speak your words and move as you suggested. It's very addictive.

This time I wanted to write a play about Yellow Springs, post Covid. So much had changed and happened, and I wanted something that felt grounding and welcoming back to the daily routine of community life. I kicked around a few ideas and was reviewing in local coffee shop (Dino's) when a similar situation occurred for the umpteenth time, something I'd seen over and over and recounted here. The absurd portion of the play came to mind all at once. It was written and edited at the local Monday writers group at another coffee shop (Emporium). The group is called "shut up and write" and is part of a national group where you do just that, you shut and write for an hour among fellow writers.

This is my best use of the ten minute limit to date. There's a full story arc, character growth, set up and denouement. It's a full play all on its own.

CHARACTERS

Mr. Twee	Stuffy, uptight business man. Adult, middle aged. Dressed business casual, but clearly not comfortable being too casual. Race irrelevant.
Future Man	Dressed in ratty clothes. Can be similar clothes to MR. TWEE, just worn out and filthy. Long beard hiding his face. Person should look vaguely like MR. TWEE in some way. Should look older than MR. TWEE, and sound older. Optionally a decrepit hoody to hide the face.
Madison	Young woman or man, referenced as a woman in the script, but gender is not important to the part and race is irrelevant. Casually dressed. Looks bored, and not enjoying her job.

TIME

Daytime. The present.

SETTING

Coffee Shop. Entranceway on one side, counter opposite. Exit behind the counter leading into back room. There is a board of drink options on the wall in front of the counter, facing the audience. The drink names are all puns. The counter has a "pad" for taking credit transactions that can rotate. There is a sign on the counter that warns of a $5 min credit purchase. There is also a bell.

NOTE: There needs to be a way FUTURE MAN can quickly enter and exit. This could include being hidden by the counter.

NOTE: The script frequently refers to Special Effects (SFX). This can be anything that covers a person entering and exiting the stage. Could be flashing lights or anything that seems out of place and unusual. The SFX purpose is to cover FUTURE MAN coming and going unseen. A bit of music or weird sound should occur during it as well, loud enough to cover entrance/exit sounds.

ACT I

SCENE 1

> At Rise:
> MR. TWEE has just entered an empty coffee shop, is at the counter, and about to order. He's staring up at the board of options and can't make up his mind. MADISON is bored, leaning on the counter, and waiting for his order.

MR. TWEE

Reading the menu slowly to himself. Muttering out loud. Stops reading the menu with a jolt of an idea. Turns to MADISON.

Oh hey! I've heard that Dave Chappell comes in here occasionally. Is that true? I'd love to meet him. I've heard he's *very* funny.

MADISON

Rolls eyes.

I'll call the townie hotline and let him know he has a visitor.

MR. TWEE

He has a hotline?

MADISON

No. Have you decided yet?

MR. TWEE

I knew what I wanted before I came in here, but now I'm not sure.

MADISON

What did you want?

MR. TWEE

I said I'm not sure.

MADISON

No, I mean when you came in here, you said you knew what you wanted then. What was that?

MR. TWEE

Just a coffee, nothing special. Maybe sugar. Dash of crème.

MADISON

I can do that.

MR. TWEE

I know, but these all sound good. I never get anything fancy. I think I want to try something new.

SFX

FUTURE MAN

Has now 'appeared', facing away from the others. He is looking around confused and lost.

MR. TWEE AND MADISON

Looking around confused by the SFX and don't notice FUTURE MAN yet.

MR. TWEE

Gracious me! What the double-l hockey sticks was that?

MADISON

Shrugs.

Old building. Does weird stuff sometimes. Be right back. Gonna go check the fuses real quick.

Exits through curtain without looking back.

MR. TWEE

What about my drink? Could you get that first?

Oh. I guess not.

FUTURE MAN

Seems to have figured something out. Is elated.

It worked!

MR. TWEE

Turns to see FUTURE MAN and notices him for the first time. He's a bit repulsed by the scruffy man.

What worked?

FUTURE MAN

Time Travel! I did it! I'm in my own past!

MR. TWEE

Time Travel? Seriously?

Thinks this is a prank. Looks around for a camera.

Is this some kind of TickTocky trend thing? A reel? Is someone filming us now?

FUTURE MAN

Oh I hope not! That would be weird. Plus, I don't remember anyone filming me, and I think I'd remember that. Yes. Yes I think I would definitely remember that. But then again, I don't remember this conversation, so maybe anything is possible!

MR. TWEE

Looking over the counter for MADISON, concerned he's alone with a crazy person.

Miss coffee person? I know what I want now! Can you come back here? Quickly? Please!

FUTURE MAN

With great alarm - No! You mustn't! You can't!

FUTURE MAN quickly inserts himself between the counter and MR. TWEE, as MR. TWEE backs away from him. FUTURE MAN puts his arms out to block the counter.

This is what I'm here to prevent! Exactly! This is the moment that changed everything!

MR. TWEE

What? Me ordering coffee?

FUTURE MAN

It's not the coffee so much, as the choice!

MR. TWEE backs further away from the crazy person.

Then I won't order anything.

FUTURE MAN

Panics.

Oh! Oh no!

SFX. FUTURE MAN is now gone. Everything else is the same.

MADISON

(OFF STAGE) Did that do anything? No? What about now?

Stage lights flicker.

MR. TWEE

I think that did it?

Looking around, wondering where FUTURE MAN went.

Could I get my drink now? I suddenly remembered I have to be somewhere right now.

SFX.

FUTURE MAN

FUTURE MAN is back, but in a different location. He's looking around confused then, elated.

It worked!

MR. TWEE

Turns to see FUTURE MAN. Clutches his heart like he's having an attack.

How did you do that? Get over there?

FUTURE MAN

Oh, I'm sorry, this must seem so strange to you from your perspective. I'm a Time Traveler. I'm here to save the future. Our Future.

MR. TWEE

Yes, I know all that. You just told me.

FUTURE MAN

Scratches his head or beard in confusion.

But I couldn't have told you. I just got here.

MR. TWEE

What are you babbling about? You were just over there a minute ago. You were screaming at me for ordering a coffee.

FUTURE MAN

Claps hands.

Ope! I know what happened! I must have already travelled here from the future and changed something. Then the circumstances that created that future never happened, so that me disappeared because they don't exist anymore. They must have done something wrong though, because our future is still awful!

MR. TWEE

Our? Our future? I don't know you. I've never seen you in my life.

FUTURE MAN

Well of course not, because I'm you from the future. It would be really crazy if you met your future self without a time machine. And time machines haven't even been invented yet. X models only went on deep discount last week, in fact. Still couldn't afford it. Even the droid model. I had to steal one from the library.

MR. TWEE

Whomever you are, you should know I'm not one to participate in pranks. And even if I were to, this is much too elaborate. It makes no sense. Why didn't you pretend to be someone else instead of me? You don't look like me at all.

FUTURE MAN

Oh! I can prove who I am. I'll tell you something that only I would know. I mean that only we would know. Ask me anything!

MR. TWEE

Fine. If that will get rid of you. What did I eat last Tuesday?

FUTURE MAN

How would I know? That was decades ago! Think of something more memorable.

MR. TWEE

This is just some trick to get my bank password isn't it? You're trying to figure out those challenge questions. Like what street did I grow up on. My mother's maiden name. That sort of thing. I'm on to you.

FUTURE MAN

It's not a trick. I swear. On my mother's name. I mean our mother's name. Please. Think of something else.

MR. TWEE

Oho! I've got you. Why did I get detention in third grade?

FUTURE MAN

What? Detention? I don't remember - oh wait - no - I do remember this! I pulled little Susie's pigtails in the desk in front of me. I wanted her to know I liked her.

MR. TWEE

Hah! Wrong! I threw a paper wad at Karen. I most certainly did not like Suzy.

FUTURE MAN

To be fair, that was forever ago. I was close.

MR. TWEE

Takes out his cellphone.

Total fraud. I won't be listening to anything you have to say. In fact, I'm calling 911.

FUTURE MAN

You can't!

MR. TWEE

Good riddance.

SFX. FUTURE MAN disappears.
SFX. FUTURE MAN reappears, facing a wall.

FUTURE MAN

Oh wow! I think it worked!

MR. TWEE

Shaking his head. Resigned.

FUTURE MAN

Turns and sees MR. TWEE and is delighted.

There you are! You won't believe this but -

MR. TWEE

You're from the future and you have some kind of issue with my getting coffee.

FUTURE MAN

Yes! How did you know -

Considers.

- we've done this before.

Shocked.

Oh! I've just now remembered this! Time travel is so freaky. It was something about lunch. I totally messed up.

MR. TWEE

If I pretend to believe you, and play along, will this be over faster?

FUTURE MAN

Ponders.

I don't remember this, so maybe so! Changes are important!

MR. TWEE

What should I order for my coffee?

FUTURE MAN

Um... Let me think. I can't tell you too much, temporal causality and all that. How about nothing fancy. Just order it black.

MR. TWEE

That's it?

FUTURE MAN

Ponders.

Positive.

SFX.

FUTURE MAN has moved to another spot.

Oh wow, it worked!

MR. TWEE

Holds up a hand to shush him.

MR. TWEE

You're from the future, and the change didn't work.

FUTURE MAN

Big sigh.

No. I'm afraid not.

MR. TWEE

Why don't you just tell me the whole thing? No more temporal causality mumbo jumbo.

FUTURE MAN

Nods and takes a deep breath. Recites this like a ranting crazy man talking to himself.

We were in a big rut and wanted badly to get out of it. You were at a breaking point. We were. I was. Whatever. A big one. You decided to order something fancy, first time in your life. You picked something way to expensive and silly. You felt like you were somebody else other than boring old you. And the drink? It was actually good. It put you in a good mood. A great mood. You were ecstatic. You jogged all the way back to the office and Laverne, from sales, she passed by your cubical. You decided to try out your new found boldness. You asked her out. Point blank. She was stunned. She said yes. You dated for weeks. You learned to dance, because she liked it. You proposed after three weeks. You were married for years. You took up painting. You had two kids. You were happy. Then one terrible day she drove the kids to swimming lessons and was killed by a drunk driver. Bam. Just like that. No one survived. You never recovered. I mean I never recovered. I ended up on the streets. I blamed it all on being too adventurous. If we were still our careful self, you would never have been hurt so badly. So very badly. Then I did the only thing that made any sense. I stole a time machine and went back in time to fix things. Then you changed your order and it got worse.

MR. TWEE

Visibly shook.

So what happened when I ordered black coffee?

FUTURE MAN

Your life was boring as hell, but you knew you had a better life you didn't choose. You were full of regret and miserable. I became a drunkard, and I ended up on the streets. During a bad bender I broke into a salvation army and stole a used time machine.

MR. TWEE

Sounds like I'm damned if I do. Damned if I don't.

FUTURE MAN

To be honest, I'm not sure what we should do. And I'm still a little buzzed. *hic*

MR. TWEE

Points to a sign on the counter that lists the special. Buckeye Mocha. Aha! Best of both worlds. I'll get the special. It's fancy but not too bold of a choice because it's an advertised special. How about that?

FUTURE MAN

Ponders.

I'm not sure.

SFX.

FUTURE MAN

Vanishes.

MR. TWEE

Waits for something to happen. After a long beat, shrugs.

Special it is.

Rings the bell.

Miss? I know what I want.

MADISON

Enters. Covered in dirt or dust, brushing it off.

Yeah? You decided finally? What is it.

MR. TWEE

Proudly.

The special. A buckeye mocha.

MADISON

Not impressed.

Ok. One Buckeye coming up.

Makes the drink.

MR. TWEE

Is looking around.

MADISON

Hands him a cup.

Here you go.

You looking for someone?

MR. TWEE

Holds up a finger. Pauses. Then nods. And is suddenly very happy and takes his drink.

Nope. Not looking for anyone.

Hands her a credit card.

MADISON

She runs it and hands it back. Then spins the pad around.

Signature please.

MR. TWEE

Pauses. Starts to write. Stops. Looks around. Smiles. Signs.

Aha! Thank you very much.

Exits front door.

MADISON

Turns the pad around.

No tip. Man I hate tourists.

FADE TO BLACK.

END.

Other Works by Scott Bachmann

Available from CorgiPress at www.corgipress.com and on Amazon in print and digital.

- Graphic Novels
    - Our Super Mom Vol 1
    - Our Super Mom Vol 2
    - Our Super Mom Vol 3
    - Hardcase Vol 1
    - Delta Dawn Vol 1
- Illustrated Books
    - Eat the Bunny Before The Bunny Eats You
    - Grass is Awful
    - Anthony Fox Does Not Believe in Ghosts
- Novels
    - The Paragon of Animals
    - To Thine Own Self Be True

www.ingramcontent.com/pod-product-compliance
Lightning Source LLC
Chambersburg PA
CBHW081632040426

42449CB00014B/3276